THE SPIRIT
OF SIMPLICITY

"Well over a half-century old, *The Spirit of Simplicity* is a remarkably approachable text, and it is still able to serve its original purpose as an entryway into Cistercian spirituality. Together with selections from St. Bernard's works, it remains a kind of classic Cistercian Life 101."

From the preface by **Abbot Elias Dietz, O.C.S.O.**
Abbey of Gethsemani

"This is a treasure of monastic spirituality that brings together the hearts, minds, and insights of two of the greatest Trappist authors of the modern era: Jean-Baptiste Chautard and Thomas Merton."

Rev. Daniel P. Horan, O.F.M.
Author of *The Franciscan Heart of Thomas Merton*

"*The Spirit of Simplicity* mines a cornerstone of Cistercian spirituality, a return to an original minimalism in *The Rule of St. Benedict* that is at once moral and aesthetic. A monastic architecture devoid of embellishments mirrors the interior work of seeking direct union with God. The early-twentieth-century elder Jean-Baptiste Chautard and a young Thomas Merton flesh out the implications for a contemplative life centered on attending to the grace of simply recognizing the 'gaze of God' within all one's experiences. Abbot Elias Dietz places these classic essays in their context and provides contemporary resources for further study and practical application."

Jonathan Montaldo
General editor of *Fons Vitae's* Thomas Merton Series

"We need simplicity now more than ever. This lost classic of Trappist spirituality unites the voices of two of the great Catholic writers of the twentieth century. It reveals how simplicity is an essential quality of a holy life. While written for monks, it is—like *The Rule of St. Benedict*—filled with wisdom for all. Read it slowly and prayerfully."

Carl McColman
Author of *Befriending Silence*

"*The Spirit of Simplicity* was one of Merton's earliest explorations of the Cisterican charism of simplicity, a subject to which he would return often. In our present age of violence, technological upheaval, and ecological vulnerability it remains eloquent and powerful."

Paul M. Pearson
Director of the Thomas Merton Center

THE SPIRIT
OF SIMPLICITY

JEAN-BAPTISTE CHAUTARD, O.C.S.O.

TRANSLATED AND ANNOTATED BY THOMAS MERTON

PREFACE AND AFTERWORD BY
ABBOT ELIAS DIETZ, O.C.S.O.
ABBEY OF GETHSEMANI

WITH ILLUSTRATIONS

AVE MARIA PRESS AVE Notre Dame, Indiana

Quotations from Holy Scripture have been translated by the authors, most often, from the Latin Vulgate into English. In a few cases, the *Douay-Rheims* has been used.

Photographs courtesy of Thomas X. Davis, O.C.S.O., Abbey of New Clairvaux, Vina, CA 96092.

Founded in 1865, Ave Maria Press is a ministry of the United States Province of Holy Cross.

www.avemariapress.com

Paperback: ISBN-13 978-1-59471-781-9

E-book: ISBN-13 978-1-59471-782-6

Cover image © dbvirago | Adobe Stock.

Cover by Angela Moody, movingimages.com.

Text design by Katherine Robinson.

Printed and bound in the United States of America.

Library of Congress Cataloging-in-Publication Data is available.

CONTENTS

PREFACE BY
ABBOT ELIAS DIETZ,
O.C.S.O.

Well over a half-century old, *The Spirit of Simplicity* is a remarkably approachable text and is still able to serve its original purpose as an entryway into Cistercian spirituality. Together with selections from St. Bernard's works, it remains a kind of classic Cistercian Life 101.

As it turned out, this unique little book also brought together two of the most significant voices in twentieth-century spirituality: Jean-Baptiste Chautard, best known for *The Soul of the Apostolate*, and Thomas Merton, who completed the project while he was working on *The Seven Storey Mountain*. So it is well worth bringing *The Spirit of Simplicity* back into print not only because of the inherent value of its contents but also because the story of its composition encapsulates a century of development in Cistercian spirituality.

For a work on simplicity, the title page of the original 1948 edition was oddly complicated:

> *The Spirit of Simplicity*
> *Characteristic of the Cistercian Order*
> *An Official Report,*
> *demanded and approved by the General Chapter*
> *Together with Texts from*
> *St. Bernard of Clairvaux*
> *on Interior Simplicity*
> *Translation and Commentary by*
> *A Cistercian Monk of Our Lady of Gethsemani*

As was customary at the time, everyone involved in the publication—apart from St. Bernard—remained anonymous. In order to fully appreciate this little work today, it will be necessary to unravel this convoluted title and to uncover its several layers of anonymity.

•   •   •

Dom Frederic Dunne, abbot of Gethsemani from 1935 to 1948, set the process in motion when, in 1945, he asked Fr. Louis (Thomas Merton) to render into English a brochure titled *The Spirit of Simplicity*, which was first published in French in 1928. There are no signs that either Dunne or Merton knew who the author of the piece was. As Merton saw it, Dom Frederic's interest in this text was consonant both with his personality and with his zeal for preserving the Cistercian tradition.[1] The fact that Dom Frederic recognized the significance of a somewhat obscure publication in French from the 1920s does say a lot about the man. The work's mixture of a forward-looking attitude toward monastic life and a strong attachment to early Cistercian ideals also characterized Dunne's approach as abbot. He was keen on making monastic life better known through all kinds of print media, from holy cards to brochures to major publications.

Merton was indebted to Dom Frederic for encouraging him to develop his writing talents, but that encouragement first took the form of putting his language skills to use. Already as a novice, he was asked to write biographical sketches of saintly early Cistercians, based mostly on Latin sources.[2] He was then put to work on a new translation of Chautard's *The Soul of the Apostolate*, published by Gethsemani in 1946. This new version had a wide readership and was later reprinted by Image Books and then by Doubleday, remaining popular well into the 1960s.

This was about the same time that Merton was asked to translate *The Spirit of Simplicity*, "which I finished in a big hurry at the end of 1945 because Father Abbot wanted it 'in print within a month,'" he writes in *The Sign of Jonas* for May 1, 1947. In the same journal entry Merton shows signs of straining under the load of numerous writing projects, including *The Seven Storey Mountain* and *The Waters of Siloe*. But not all this work was imposed on him. Merton's journal note concludes, "Fortunately, Father Abbot's injunctions are always good-natured enough to be quite vague and flexible. He gets an idea and communicates it to me and I happily accept it, but it is understood that if I cannot do it I will say so and it will be dropped." In the case of *The Spirit of Simplicity*, Merton used the abbot's latitude to expand the project and make it his own. Dom Frederic wanted the pamphlet in English; what he got was considerably more.

There is no telling what Merton thought of the text in question, since he consistently refers to it detachedly as "the report." He intervenes more often in the footnotes than one would normally expect of a translator. Most of these additions provide helpful information to the reader, but some are slightly polemic (e.g., n. 40 on p. 28 and n. 49 on p. 30), and on one occasion he objects to a statement in the report (n. 7 on p. 38). Where he weighs in most heavily and with some pique in these notes is on the topic of architecture (n. 44 on p. 29 and n. 52 on p. 32). The addition of a series of twelve photographs of Cistercian monasteries, found in this volume between parts 1 and 2, was no doubt his initiative.

. . .

"Report" is an unfortunate but understandable title for the original text, given the fact that it was commissioned by the General Chapter of 1925. To set the scene for this chapter, it is helpful to recall that what is now known as the Order of Cistercians of the Strict Observance (O.C.S.O.) was formed in 1892 by the merging of three Strict Observance congregations. This move, made at the urging of Pope Leo XIII, had the advantage of uniting a large number of monasteries with similar outlook and customs. At the same time, it had the disadvantage of officially dividing the Cistercian family by the creation of a separate entity more familiarly referred to as the Trappists.

In the 1920s the abbots of this still young order undertook the delicate task of updating its book of customs, the *Usages*. Although the ancient predecessor of the *Usages* (the twelfth-century *Ecclesiastica Officia*) dealt mostly with liturgical matters, the identity of the various Strict Observance monasteries had come to reside in a much-expanded body of usages that regulated all aspects of monastic life, often in minute detail. Leading members of the order's General Chapter sensed the danger of formalism in this approach and began to feel the need for a return to the original sources of Cistercian life and spirituality.

It was in this context that the General Chapter of 1925 commissioned Dom Jean-Baptiste Chautard (1858–1935) to write a text that could serve as a preface to the *Usages*. His task, according to the minutes of that chapter, was to recall to the monasteries of the order "the spirit of simplicity on which our early Fathers insisted when they promulgated the *Exordium Parvum*." This latter text (referred to in Merton's translation as the *Little Exordium*) is a narrative account interspersed with official documents that tells the story of the foundation of Cîteaux and its gradual expansion into a network of related monasteries.

Although *The Spirit of Simplicity* often mentions Stephen (third abbot of Cîteaux, a native of England, where he was known as Harding) as the author of the *Exordium Parvum*, more recent scholarship has shown it to be a hybrid text, put together in stages, only parts of which can be assigned to Stephen. In any case, it is striking to note that in 1925 the General Chapter was beginning to apply what Vatican Council II later proposed as the guiding principles for the renewal of religious life: rediscovery of the founders' intentions and renewed contact with the specific spirituality of the order as expressed in its earliest sources.

Dom Jean-Baptiste Chautard was a natural choice for this work. A leading figure in the order since the turn of the century, he belonged to a generation of abbots who saw a need to shift the focus away from the details of external observance to the specific spirituality that was meant to give Cistercian life its shape. This was no small undertaking. On one hand, the Trappist reform led by Abbot de Rancé in the seventeenth century tended to emphasize the desert tradition and other sources of inspiration such as St. John Climacus. On the other hand, monasteries were inclined to maintain their specific customs externally but to cultivate the interior life along the lines of the predominant spirituality of the day, marked especially by the writings of St. Ignatius of Loyola and St. Francis de Sales. Chautard and his contemporaries perceived the need to overcome this loss of contact with their own tradition by returning to the Rule of Benedict and to early Cîteaux as their primary sources of inspiration.

Although it is natural to identify Dom Jean-Baptiste Chautard with *The Soul of the Apostolate*, the published work for which he is best known, that book was not, strictly speaking, a monastic undertaking. His intended audience was people engaged in the active apostolate, and he took his inspiration from a wide range of Christian authors. Its first version was written at the request of Marie-Ignace Melin, mother superior of a new order of religious sisters who taught catechism in the suburbs of Paris. Its origins are reflected in the title of the first edition (1907), *The Catechetical Apostolate and the Interior Life: Martha and Mary.* Later versions of the book intended for an even broader audience bear the more familiar title *The Soul of the Apostolate*, which has become something of a classic in spiritual literature. Pope Pius X is said to have kept it on his nightstand and Pope emeritus Benedict XVI cited it during his visit to Lourdes in 2008.

A skilled administrator with many responsibilities in his own monastery and elsewhere in the order, Chautard was not naturally inclined to write for publication. When he did put pen to paper, it was in response to the needs of the moment. For instance, he produced a number of articles from 1914 to 1918 for a wartime publication whose aim was to help mobilized priests maintain the ideals of their vocation. Most of his monastic teaching was conveyed informally to his own community in chapter. He nonetheless wrote several short works on the Rule of St. Benedict, St. Bernard, and Cistercian life. *The Spirit of Simplicity*, written on request in response to a specific need, is his most significant monastic work.

In the biographical note on Dom Chautard accompanying his translation of *The Soul of the Apostolate*, Thomas Merton does not mention *The Spirit of Simplicity*. Perhaps he was unaware that Chautard had written it, or perhaps he wished to respect the anonymity of a document mandated by the General Chapter. Whatever his estimation of "the report," Merton clearly thought there was room for a fuller treatment of its topic and opted to add part 2, with excerpts from St. Bernard and commentary. It is good to keep in mind that in 1945 Chautard's text was far from new and belonged to a previous generation. Paradoxically, however, Merton's work in part 2, with its long, complex sentences and scholastic theological terms, now seems more dated than the direct and practical 1928 report.

Merton's stated purpose was to present selections from St. Bernard that "will give us the massive dogmatic foundations upon which the Cistercian doctrine of simplicity is built as upon granite." Along with this weighty image came a certain heaviness of presentation. He was, after all, a student at the time, and the twentieth-century revival of scholastic theology—which postdated Chautard's formative years—was in full swing. Moreover, the influence of Étienne Gilson's 1934 book *The Mystical Theology of St. Bernard* is quite noticeable.

Although part 2 of *The Spirit of Simplicity* is far from reader friendly, and although Merton considered his contribution "confused and weak,"[3] it was nonetheless an impressive accomplishment for a relatively young monk. With good pedagogical instinct, he wanted to complement the report's focus on sketchy early documents with the well-rounded teaching of the abbot of Clairvaux. In doing so, he demonstrates an impressive knowledge of St. Bernard's writings.[4] We see here the makings of the excellent novice master he became some years later.

In conclusion, then, at the heart of this book is the story of the rediscovery of Cistercian spirituality in the first half of the twentieth century. The choice of topic, approach, and author comes from the forward-looking General Chapter of 1925. The tone and spirit of the text come from Dom Jean-Baptiste Chautard, a key representative of his generation. It was an abbot of the next generation, Dom Frederic Dunne of Gethsemani, who recognized the long-term importance of the work and wanted to make it available to the English-speaking world. His chosen translator was none other than Thomas Merton, who, not content with a mere translation of a brochure-length report, stepped in both as annotator and coauthor, thus turning *The Spirit of Simplicity* into the influential little book it became.

Sources and References

Throughout *The Spirit of Simplicity*, in both parts 1 and 2, there are many endnotes with references to sources, along with a variety of other annotations. In part 1, it is important to distinguish between the original notes of Chautard's texts (written by Chautard) and Merton's own numerous and sometimes lengthy translator's notes. The latter are indicated, in this edition, by the same method that Merton used in 1948: with a simple "Translator" after each one.

Given the time of writing (the 1920s for Chautard and the 1940s for Merton), many cited sources are now obscure and need to be brought up to date. Moreover, both authors presumed that their audiences were familiar with Latin. In order to increase the book's usefulness for a twenty-first-century readership, some adaptations have been made in the endnotes. Scriptural and patristic references have been brought in line with standard practice, but it should be noted that the Vulgate numbering has been retained for references to the psalms. Where necessary, translations of Latin passages are given between square brackets.

The most significant updating needed has to do with references to the early Cistercian documents. In *The Spirit of Simplicity*, two nineteenth-century editions are cited simply as Nomasticon[5] (often abbreviated to Nom.) and Guignard.[6] These references will be retained for the sake of anyone who wants to consult the actual Latin editions used by the authors. Where possible, however, a more complete and up-to-date reference to an English translation will be added in square brackets. For these additional references, a list of abbreviations is provided with the notes.

FOREWORD BY
THOMAS MERTON

In speaking of simplicity in the spiritual life, it is well to get rid of all purely dramatic or fanciful or sentimental concepts of this virtue at the very outset. *Simplicity* is a word that has too many meanings—often very vague meanings—when applied to the interior life. It generally conjures up a picture of some ideally, romantically "simple" character: a personage endowed, perhaps, with not much brains, but with a nice, kind face and a beautiful, ingenuous disposition, a sweet attractiveness of manner that is described in another vague and much misused word: *childlike*. The two terms are coupled together, and thus we hear much about "childlike simplicity." Sometimes the expression really means something definite: humility, obedience, charity. At other times it means little more than natural charm.

Now simplicity is one of the outstanding characteristics of Cistercian spirituality and of Cistercian saintliness. Indeed, the experience of many monks will verify the fact that when members of our order are seen to grow and progress in sanctity among us, the chief characteristic which they acquire is this simplicity.

Going further below the surface, entering into the fundamentals of our Rule, our usages, our ascetic practices, our traditions, and the teaching of our fathers, we find that the deeper we go the deeper and more significant a concept of simplicity do we obtain: and this concept is always more and more intimately bound up with the very essence of Cistercian spirituality.

Keenly conscious of this fact, and of the no less important truth that this simplicity depends, for its very existence, on the basic legislation about poverty, fasting, enclosure, silence, etc., laid down by our fathers, the General Chapter of 1925 suggested and approved the official report on the subject which we here present in a new translation from the French. This report, which comprises the first half of the present book, expresses the views of the General Chapter and therefore of the order on the meaning of Cistercian simplicity and, above all, on the necessity of maintaining it by generous and faithful adherence to the spirit of the early legislation laid down particularly in the *Little Exordium*.

As the official report deals principally with external simplicity, that is, with simplicity in clothing, buildings, the liturgy, and so on, we have considered it worthwhile to add a second section devoted to a brief outline of the doctrine of St. Bernard on interior simplicity or, to be more exact, on the importance played by interior simplicity in the ascetical teaching of the great Cistercian Doctor of the Church, as expressed in four typical groups of quotations from his most important works.

This will, no doubt, provide a suitable and helpful complement to the official report that deals with interior simplicity more briefly and without any special reference to Cistercian sources.

We may remind the reader that the demand of the General Chapter for such a report implies an earnest desire that all members of the order apply themselves to study and examination of conscience on the subject which may, perhaps, have hitherto escaped them, due to ignorance or lack of contact with the sources of Cistercian spirituality. Are we really true to the spirit of the *Little Exordium* in its interpretation of the Rule of St. Benedict?

It is well within the compass of the desires of the General Chapter to add the pages we have compiled on interior simplicity according to St. Bernard, and the perusal of these ideas from the pen of the saint who is for us *par excellence* our commentator of the Rule and master in the spiritual life will help us to a more intelligent understanding and practice of the principles laid down by St. Stephen Harding.

We may sum up the teaching of St. Bernard and of the *Little Exordium* in a few brief words by saying that, for them, simplicity consisted in *getting rid of everything that did not help the monk to arrive at union with God by the shortest possible way.*

And the shortest possible way to arrive at union with God, who is Love, is by loving him, in himself, and in our brethren.

Consequently, simplicity meant for our fathers the discarding of two classes of things: first, everything that was opposed to charity, to the love of God; that is not only mortal sin but all the pleasures and vanities and useless occupations of the world whether they might be in themselves harmless or openly noxious. But second, and this is much more important, for it is something that monks have often failed to grasp quite clearly: simplicity also meant for them the *discarding of means of getting to God that were less direct,* less perfect, less effective, even though they might, indeed, bring us to union with him indirectly and in a roundabout way. Hence, the Cistercians gave up many active works which, though very useful and necessary in themselves, were only *indirect* means to perfect union with God, compared to a life of silence, prayer, penance, sacrifice, and contemplation.[1]

This explains why the ancient Cistercians were so drastic in eliminating nonessential decorations from their churches: these things might be means to elevate the mind to God, but they were *less perfect,* less effective means. The monk would soon outgrow all such expedients and enter upon the path of more interior, affective, and contemplative prayer, and as soon as he did so, this wealth of decorations would serve rather to distract him than to unite him with God, if he noticed them at all: and on the other hand if he did not notice them, what use would they be?

This definition may tell us something of simplicity: but it leaves out one most important point, which is the fact that all this takes place because the intellect and the will of the monk seek one object alone, God as he is in himself, not merely as reflected in his creatures or in his gifts. The Cistercians became simple because they had seen too many monks become so entranced with the gifts of God that they clung to them and turned away from their Giver and Creator.

A few words of the friend and biographer of St. Bernard, Blessed William of Saint Thierry, will help to give us a good general notion of this simplicity, before we turn to the pages of the official report on the subject.

This Cistercian theologian explains that we can know nothing naturally except through the medium of our senses. When we come to turn our minds and wills to objects that are above the senses and especially to God who is infinitely beyond the comprehension of our highest intellectual faculties in their natural state, there are two courses open to us. We can proceed according to our own lights: but, since these are worse than useless, in these higher orders, we only become fools by doing so. This is the way of pride, *stultitia*—stupidity. The other path we can take is simplicity. This implies a humble and obedient subjection to God's own authority and to those whom he delegates to guide us, in order that we may be safely led to him, in our blindness, traveling as we do on an unknown way that is to us impenetrable darkness.

"When the soul thus turns to God," says William of Saint Thierry, "holy simplicity is the result: and this simplicity may be defined as a *constant and unchanging desire for one object and him alone (eadem semper circa idem voluntas)*, as was the case with holy Job, who was called a man simple and upright, and fearing God. In the strict sense, simplicity is the perfect conversion of the will to God, asking one thing of God, and desiring that alone, and not going forth and multiplying itself in the world.[2]

"In another sense simplicity means genuine humility; that is, a virtue which seeks the approval of conscience rather than the applause of fame, and according to which the simple man is not afraid to be thought a fool by the world, in order that he may be wise unto God."[3]

Since the two following parts of this book will be devoted almost entirely to an explanation and development of the thoughts contained in these lines, we may pass on at once to them.

PART 1

THE SPIRIT OF SIMPLICITY: CHARACTERISTIC OF THE CISTERCIAN ORDER

DOM JEAN-BAPTISTE CHAUTARD, O.C.S.O.

INTRODUCTION

The variety in the spirit of the different saints canonized by the Church, and the diversity among religious orders all manifest the great wealth of the spirit of the Gospel: one single form of human living would not by itself suffice to express it.

And so the Rule of St. Benedict is an authentic compendium of the precepts and counsels of the Gospels, which it adapts to the needs of a large number of souls who are called to become saints. It is easy to see, from this, why God has raised up not only numerous saints to exemplify, by their lives, the spirit of the Patriarch of the Monks of the West, but also a diversity of religious institutes for the same purpose. The latter, whether as branches or reforms, have been able to emphasize, in their observances, one or another special point contained in the Rule: this has been quite legitimate, as long as they have remained faithful to the spirit of the blessed patriarch and have not perverted, in some subtle manner, the slightest detail of the meaning of his prescriptions wherever the spirit of the venerable legislator is expressed in them.

Outstanding among all these institutes, by reason of a most scrupulous fidelity to the real meaning of St. Benedict, were the early Cistercians.

The founders of Cîteaux drew their inspiration from that eminently simple source, the spirit of the Rule, and therefore they themselves remained simple. They gloried in nothing but the fact that they kept the limpid water of that blessed fount untainted. So, if we can say that simplicity is one of the characteristics of our order, this is the reason why.

The truth of the matter is that our saintly forefathers reduced everything to the following threefold objective:

1. to identify their love of the Rule with their love for Jesus Christ;
2. to give themselves loyally to the study of the full meaning of the Rule; and

3. to throw themselves wholeheartedly into the task of carrying it out to the letter.[1]

Generosity without reserve in everything that the Rule lays down: but nothing that the Rule does not prescribe—the whole Cistercian life is summed up in those words. Simplicity is here expressed in the terms: "No more, and no less." In other words: no subtractions that might lead to that condition of tepidity and negligence which were emphasized by Hugh, the papal legate, as the objects of the aversion of our saintly founders. But, on the other hand, any additions to the Rule, inspired by sectarian zeal *sub specie recti* [with the pretext of being right] are also prohibited. That was why the entire order rose up as a man, in spite of its veneration for St. Bernard's successor at Clairvaux, Abbot Fastrede, the moment that he, on becoming abbot of Cîteaux, attempted to add to the observances, and thus modify the program which all of them had vowed to observe at their profession.

The only reason why St. Stephen established the General Chapters and proposed to the one held in 1119[2] his admirable Charter of Charity the obligatory basis of the deliberations of the General Chapters for all time, was to insure the continuance of this clearly determined program, and to maintain, in peace and charity, the interpretation of the Rule that had been arrived at in the early days of Cîteaux.

Even after the order's golden age, Providence made marvelous use of these chapters to rekindle the sacred fire by calling the sons of Cîteaux back to the spirit of their first fathers. Sometimes the one presiding would throw light upon one or another of the basic ideas of the Rule in his exhortations, full of solid truth—and, indeed, we are well aware to what extent the fathers attending the chapter have been privileged, in this respect, since the fusion of the three congregations [in 1892]. On other occasions, the venerable assembly has invited study of some particular question, with a view to reviving and strengthening the exercise of some virtue throughout the order by means of a renewed fidelity to some observance dear to our fathers.

And so, the General Chapter of 1925 has focused our attention on the spirit of simplicity, that truly monastic virtue, forgetfulness of which at a certain period so disastrously accelerated the decline of our order.

1

INTERIOR
SIMPLICITY

Only a very inadequate idea of exterior simplicity can be arrived at if we do not trace it back to its true source: *interior simplicity*. Without this, our resolution to practice exterior simplicity would be without light, without love: it would remain too superficial, too dry to be anything but a feeble, impoverished temporary thing, lacking all vital connection with its principle and its end.

St. Benedict has a phrase that sums up interior simplicity: *Si vere Deum quaerit.*[1] It is nothing but the right intention of the soul, directed toward its last end: God. Here we have the characteristic of the monk: a man absorbed in one exclusive ideal: union with God.

In simplicitate cordis quaerite Illum—"Seek him in the simplicity of your heart" (Ws 1:1). This, says St. Bernard, is demanded by the perfectly simple nature of God.[2] The monk, turning away from multiplicity, back to unity, tears himself away from created things, among which he has been scattered by the breakage resulting from his original fall, and returns to his principle, God, sovereign and unchangeable unity.[3]

Grace will make every monk, who does not stop somewhere along the road in his quest for God, a *contemplative* in the sense in which the Church likes to apply this name to the monastic order. *Optimam partem elegit:* he has chosen the best part, and contemplation is, in the divine plan, the crown of the life of every monk. Contemplation: that is to say, a *simple* gazing upon God, a gaze that is fused with love, and which is the prelude to that *consummation in unity*[4] and, therefore, perfect simplicity which is the beatific vision.

Love is "the power that realizes unity."[5] It first produces unity in the soul, and then it makes the soul *one same spirit with God* (1 Cor 6:17).[6]

"He who finds all things in the supreme Unity," says the author of the *Imitation of Christ*, "and who reduces all to that Unity, and sees all in that Unity, will ever preserve his heart unmoved, and will dwell in peace in the bosom of his God."[7]

This is the lesson given by the master in that passage of the Gospel which is so dear to the contemplative orders, where, calling the soul that has poured itself out in activity back to peace, he says: *Turbaris erga plurima* ["Thou art solicitous about many things"] and invites her to enter upon the way of interior simplicity: one thing is necessary, *unum est necessarium*.

The monk is a man of oneness, simplicity: his very name declares it.[8]

According to St. Denis, one of the masters of St. Thomas, monks got their name from "that life indivisible and one, in which the holy union of all their powers leads them to oneness, even to the point of deiform unity. . . ."[9] Just as the Christian engages himself, at baptism, according to Denis's forceful expression, "to tend, with all his powers, to the One"[10] the monk declares, in his consecration of himself, that he renounces "every kind, every imaginable form of divided life. . . ."[11] He must unify himself by contact with the One, and recollect himself in holy simplicity."[12]

And again Denis says: "It is impossible to have part, at the same time, in things that are absolutely contrary to one another. No one can cling steadfastly to the One and lead a divided life: it is therefore necessary to gain one's freedom and become detached from everything that destroys unity."[13]

Therefore, whoever keeps "his eyes open to the light that makes us godlike,"[14] to use St. Benedict's words, and "hastens toward our heavenly country"[15] "goes straight to his Creator."[16] And therefore, for such a one, everything that does not lead to this end diverts him from it, and must be sacrificed. The monk detaches himself from everything that might weigh him down and bind him to the earth. He wants to be *simple*, not *mixed up* with the things that are below him.[17]

Thus, as St. Bernard says, "loving God with all its being, despising the earth, looking up to heaven, making use of this world as if it used it not, the soul distinguishes *by an inward and spiritual sense of touch between those things which are for its use, and those which are for its enjoyment,* so that it grants only a passing attention to the things that are, themselves, passing, *simply because it is necessary, and in the measure in which it is necessary,* while embracing in an eternal desire the things that are eternal" (Sermon 50 on the Canticle of Canticles).

The lines we sing in the hymn for Prime point out the way for us to follow in this program of detachment which leads to the glorification of God:

Mundi per absenentiam,
Ipsi canamus gloriam.

"And, purified by abstinence, may we sing to him a hymn of glory."

Denis says: "It is necessary for us to be brought back from what is manifold to what is one by the power of divine unity, and that we glorify only the divinity, total and single, as the One, the author of all things."[18]

This austere concern with which the monk works to remove every obstacle that stands in the way of his progress in union with God has, as one of its consequences, *exterior simplicity* in all his conduct, in the use he makes of created goods, in his clothing, nourishment, housing, his occupations, and all his relations with other men. All of these will be characterized by restraint, poverty, humility, modesty, recollection, and the spirit of solitude, of enclosure, and of silence.

It would be a joy to listen to someone like St. Francis de Sales on this subject. He would compare all these virtues to the various oils blended together by the artistry of a skilled distiller of perfumes, all having different scents which blend to produce an aroma with its own distinctive charm: simplicity in our every action.[19]

So, indeed, "by a vigorous aspiring to the One, being strong in casting aside all that is opposed to him, everything that was in disorder becomes ordered, all that was formless acquires a form in the rays of a life that is all light."[20]

Returning to God "by the labor of obedience"[21] the Cistercians were to "follow the Rule as their master"[22] since it was, for them, the expression of God's will, and so they would animate and purify, through simplicity of intention, these virtues which direct our outward conduct, by reducing them to the love which seeks to imitate our beloved Savior: for love it is that makes unity.[23] According to the prescription of the Rule they would "hold nothing dearer to them than Christ"[24] and they would "renounce themselves to follow him."[25] They would give themselves entirely to Jesus Christ, and he would become the exemplar and model for everything that they did. Men would be able to say of them: *Neminem viderunt nisi solum Jesum* ["They saw no one but only Jesus" (Mt 17:8)].

Thus a religious who is really simple will be able to say, under the impulsion of the Holy Spirit: *Scio Deus meus quod simplicitatem diligas, unde et ego in simplicitate cordis mei laetus obtuli universa* ["My God, I know Thou lovest simplicity, wherefore I also, rejoicing in the simplicity of my heart, offered Thee all things" (1 Chr 29:17)].

This simplicity of outlook in the soul of each individual monk is what produces that unity in the monastery which St. Benedict so earnestly desired. St. Bernard, too, exhorts us to desire it in these moving words: "Among us also, brothers, let all our souls be truly united together; let our hearts make but one heart by loving the same One, seeking the same One, clinging to him together, and let them all be filled with like sentiments toward one another."[26]

2

BEING TRUE TO OUR IDEALS

Have we taken note of the fact that the Church selects the same oration for the feasts of St. Benedict and of our father St. Stephen? Surely her purpose in doing so is to bring home to us the identity in the spirit of these two saints, who saw eye to eye in their perfect simplicity. More than that, the Church wants to increase our esteem for that spirit by pointing out its identity with the action of the Holy Ghost himself upon these two founders: *excita SPIRITUM . . . ut EODEM nos repleti studeamus . . . in unitate EJUSDEM Spiritus Sancti. . . .* The prayer is: *Excita Domine in Ecclesia tua Spiritum cui beatus Benedictus [Stephanus] abbas servivet, ut eodem nos repleti studeamus amare quod amavit et opere exercere quod docuit. Per Dominum . . . in unitate ejusdem,* etc. "Arouse, O Lord, in thy Church, the Spirit whom St. Benedict [Stephen], abbot, served, that we, being also filled with the same Spirit, may love what he loved and do the works which he taught us to perform. Through our Lord . . . who liveth and reigneth in the unity of the same Spirit, etc."

Truly, it is the Holy Spirit that chooses, prepares, and directs the foundation of every order and gives to it (as he also does to every reform worthy of the name) a special character. It is his wisdom that has conceived a very precise plan in each case. And so we can logically conclude that the perfection of

11

an order will be *proportionate to its conformity with the spirit of its founders. Quantum . . . tantum.*

Only those institutions which have preserved their original spirit, or have found their way back to it, receive from God the power to produce saints worthy of being proposed by the Church to the worship of all the faithful. But when an order does not drink deeply enough at the source of living waters which sprang up out of the heart of God for its foundation, God may well give it brilliant scholars, and even fervent religious. But his wisdom usually refrains from exalting them by raising them to the honors of the altar, lest he give the impression that he means to consecrate their deficiencies with his full approval.

But when an order has really gone off the rails in some fundamental issue of the primitive spirit, we can almost hear its founder thundering down from heaven this text of Jeremiah: *Dereliquerunt fontem aquae vivae, et foderunt sibi cisternas dissipatas*—"They have forsaken the fountain of living waters, and dug for themselves broken cisterns" (Jer 2:13). If you cut off the stream from its source, it will dry up, says St. Cyprian.[1]

It is therefore a matter of obligation for us Cistercians to return often to the study of our ancient Rule, so that we may never forget the fundamental spirit of our reform to which the Church thought it not amiss to grant the title of a true religious order.

The liturgy goes further and urges us to ask yet more: *Perfice pium in nobis sanctae religionis affectum, et ad obtinendam tuae gratiae largitatem* . . . [Lord, bring to perfection the grace of our monastic profession and . . . grant us the full bounty of your grace].[2] We are exhorted to keep on *progressing* in the love of our order and of our fathers, in order that this love may win us a copious flood of graces. And here it is a question not only of an affective, but an effective love: a love that will translate itself into generous efforts to put into practice everything that is characteristic of our order.

"Never lose sight of our first fathers, the founders of our holy order," wrote the pope, Blessed Eugene III, to the General

Chapter of 1150. He already felt uneasy at the thought that fervor might diminish and, with it, the love of all that he had admired and lived as a humble monk at Clairvaux.

Many other popes also invited the Cistercians, and in the most direct of language, to drink from the source of ancient Cîteaux. These appeals are recalled to mind in solemn terms by these words addressed in the schema of the [First] Vatican Council to all orders in general. "We strongly urge the heads of orders and all religious to be most solicitous in keeping to their observances and regular discipline, and to show themselves to be religious not only by their habit, but *by the virtues and spirit which animated their holy founders.*"[3]

Among these founders, God raised up St. Stephen and gave him not only the task of leading us back by his example to the practice of the holy Rule, like St. Alberic and St. Robert, but also to establish regular visitations and General Chapters. These institutions not only made the order of Cîteaux a true religious order, but obliged us, in some sense, to follow the advice given by the Holy Spirit in the fifteenth chapter of Proverbs: *Bibe aquam de cisterna tua*—drink water from thine own cistern. And should we have forgotten to do so, they would furnish a reminder.

St. Stephen looked ahead. He knew that Satan would sooner or later begin to cajole the passions or transform himself into an angel of light in order to turn the Cistercians away from the clear-cut ideals of which God, by miracles, had revealed himself to be the author. Here are a few words from the Charter of Charity which bear witness to the farsighted prudence of the holy abbot: "[S]o that if they should ever turn aside from their first resolve and from (which God forbid!) the observance of the holy Rule, they may once more, by our care and vigilance, be led to bring their lives once more into conformity with it."[4] Not only did the General Chapter of 1119—an assembly that included more than one saint among its number—make this concern of St. Stephen's its own, but Callixtus II, by his bull of December 23, 1119, approved the work as coming from the hand of God. His words were: "We confirm, with the seal of our authority, the divine work which you have undertaken."[5]

Of course, it is true that the Charter of Charity aimed, first of all, at preventing anything that was contrary to the holy Rule. But after that it went on to prescribe that all the houses of the order should interpret the Rule in exactly the same way as the first fathers of Cîteaux. This charter, drawn up in view of the creation of an administrative organism that would insure this result, makes use of language so clear that a commentary would fall short of its luminous precision. "So now it is our wish," says the charter, "and it is *our express command* to them, that they observe the Rule of St. Benedict in all things *just as it is observed at the new monastery. Let them not interpret the text of the holy Rule in any new sense*: but let them understand it and keep it in the very same sense as our predecessors and holy fathers, the monks of the new monastery (i.e., St. Robert and St. Alberic and those of their companions who had by that time died), *and in which we ourselves, at this day, understand it and keep it.*"[6]

Only a spirit of faith, humility, and renunciation can keep alive in our hearts true loyalty to the principle of essential simplicity which made our fathers leave Molesme. This same spirit must also inspire us to study what meaning our fathers found in the Rule, and what were the particular observances which they instituted in order to make the spirit of simplicity, which they found in St. Benedict, an actuality in their lives.

3

SIMPLICITY IN THE *LITTLE EXORDIUM*

The close fidelity of this document to the Rule meant that simplicity became the outstanding characteristic of Cistercian monasticism.

There is nothing in the Charter of Charity to tell us precisely how our fathers understood and practiced (*intellexerunt et tenuerunt*) the holy Rule. Where, then, is one to turn in order to find our own good "homemade bread" for the nourishment of his soul? Where are we to look for genuine evidence concerning the interpretation of the Rule in the early days of Cîteaux? Valuable as the collection of "*Consuetudines*"[1] may be, in this respect, the *Little Exordium* is, without any doubt, the more informative document, since in it are laid down the *essentials* of the Cistercian reform. The *Consuetudines*, on the other hand, deal rather with details of the liturgy, or points of monastic observance, or the resume of General Chapters following the time of St. Stephen. These regulations were, perhaps, drawn up in part at the same time as the Charter of Charity, but this assertion is no better than a probability. On the other hand, it is clearly evident that the *Little Exordium* relates practices that took effect as early as the time of St. Alberic. Besides this, the first papal approbation of the *Consuetudines* that can be accepted with any degree of certainty came as late as 1180, while there is not the slightest doubt that the *Little Exordium* was approved by Pope Callixtus II at the same time as the Charter of Charity—that is, in 1119.

1119! By that time, how much had happened: and yet it was only a few short years since 1112 when St. Stephen, disconcerted and confused by the deaths of so many of his sons, by the complete lack of vocations, and by the temporal destitution of his abbey, had begun to ask himself in deepest humility if, perhaps, the program of essential simplicity upon which the fathers of Cîteaux had embarked might not be an illusion of fervor, and had prayed God to make known his will in the matter.

Less than eight years later, about the end of 1119, he could remark, in the concluding lines of his *Little Exordium*, that there were twelve daughter or granddaughter houses in the family of Cîteaux, and bless God for the flourishing state of this abbey even in material things. "This church, Cîteaux, beheld an increase of lands, vineyards, pastures, and granges."[2] But he added at once the reason for his joy: "And all this was without detriment to the religious spirit: *nec religione decrevit.*"

In 1120 the saint beheld a still greater surge of vitality in the Cistercian family tree.

The *Exordium Cisterciensis Coenobii* did not acquire the name of *Little Exordium (Exordium Parvum)* until about a century after it was written, and the purpose of the title was to distinguish it from the *Exordium Magnum* (Great Exordium), which was not finished until the beginning of the thirteenth century.[3]

In writing down the information it contains, for the pope, who was in France at the time, St. Stephen had three ends in view:

1. To give an historical account of the origin of Cîteaux.
2. To show that the community rested on a firm canonical foundation.

3. Finally, and this is what chiefly concerns us here, he intended to submit the principal observances of the Cistercians to papal consideration and approval, in order that they might thereby become a matter of obligation.

Under the title: "Regulations of the monks of Cîteaux, who came from Molesme," chapter 15 of the *Little Exordium* begins as follows: "This abbot [Alberic] and his brethren established in this place the observance of the Rule of St. Benedict, and unanimously resolved to remain faithful to it."[4]

The statutes to which chapter 17 refers were drawn up while St. Alberic was abbot, and were promulgated under St. Stephen.

Therefore, the disciplinary sections of the *Little Exordium* give us a clear and authentic picture of the monastic ideal which God had begotten in the souls of our first founders. It not only shows us with what consummate prudence they acted, but also constitutes an official, legal document, principally on account of its approbation by the Holy See. Without doubt, the main lines of the *Little Exordium* were traced out before our fathers left Molesme. Then, on the other hand, St. Bernard had been an abbot since 1115, and he was present at the General Chapter of 1119. Consequently, when we read these statutes we are listening not only to St. Alberic and St. Stephen, but to St. Robert and to the holy abbot of Clairvaux.

M. Guignard writes in his masterly preface to his book *Les Monuments Primitifs de la Règle Cistercienne*,[5] "If the Charter of Charity laid down the lines on which the new order was to be governed, it was none the less necessary to give the newborn religious institute its *own particular spirit, its special character*. For each religious order has some form proper to itself by which it is *set apart* from all others. "But," he concludes, "the thing that was henceforth to *distinguish* Cistercians from all other monks was to be this body of primitive regulations (in the *Little Exordium*) which concerned themselves with the manner in which the Rule was to be observed."[6]

Now it is not the purpose of this present report to examine the question whether it may ever become possible to get back to certain points in strict conformity with the letter of the *Little Exordium*. All the General Chapter requires is that we make use of the *Little Exordium* and other material of St. Bernard's time in order to show in a few pages calculated to be of service to the monasteries of our order, what great importance our first fathers attached to the *spirit of simplicity*. And then, to point out how, with great energy for a century and a half, and with less in the century that followed, and still, in subsequent ages, how sudden recrudescences of the old spirit always kept reaffirming in our order the will to maintain this spirit of simplicity, or to get back to it with true fidelity if it happened to decline.

A few words from the *Little Exordium* about the statutes prior to the death of St. Alberic give us deep insight into the soul of that saint: "New soldiers of Christ, and poor as he was poor, even while they disdained the goods of this world, they asked themselves how they were going to find anything to live on, and how they would fulfill the duties of hospitality to rich and poor who, according to the Rule, were to be received as Christ himself if they presented themselves at the monastery."[7] *New soldiers of Christ, and poor as he was poor!* It sounds like St. Francis of Assisi and his marriage with holy poverty, and thereby with the simplicity of Christ Jesus.

And this is the place for a very *important observation*.

With each prohibition or prescription, our founders were very anxious to give a reason based on some indication of the spirit of St. Benedict in the Rule or in the life of the holy legislator. Let us hear what the *Exordium* has to say: "They had never read anywhere in the Rule or in the life of St. Benedict that the great teacher had ever owned parishes, altars, rights to customary offerings, burial dues, or tithes of other men, bakeries, mills, farms (tenanted by seculars), or serfs. Still less did they find that women had been admitted to the enclosure, or that any outsider had been buried therein, except his sister. And so they repudiated all these sources of revenue."[8]

Our fathers made no laws except under the impulsion of the fundamental spirit of simplicity, the desire to return to the Rule pure and simple: "Faithful to their promise," says the *Exordium*, "they unanimously decided to establish the Rule of St. Benedict in this place, and to keep it faithfully."[9]

Still in the same fifteenth chapter of the *Exordium* we read:

> When our blessed father St. Benedict teaches that the monk must become a total stranger to the things of this world, he clearly signifies that all these things (the material concerns enumerated above) cannot possibly find a place in the hearts or actions of the true monk, who is bound to live up to the strict etymological meaning of his name by flying far from all such worldly affairs.[10]

The spirit of Cîteaux is a spirit of simplicity: that means, a spirit of sincerity, of truth. Since our fathers had promised God, in their profession, that they would keep the Rule of St. Benedict, they undertook the task of reform with the sole purpose of making good their promise.[11]

The reason why they set out to keep the Rule as it was written, without the "ifs" and evasions of the commentators, the reason why they wanted to live as monks "according to the strict etymological meaning of [their] name," was that they were true sons of St. Benedict. They had inherited his spirit—the spirit which demands that the thoughts in the mind should harmonize with the words on the lips when we sing in choir (*ut mens nostra concordet voci nostrae*)[12] and that we should all be, in reality, what we are supposed to be (*semper meminisse debet [abbas] quod dicitur, et nomen majoris factis implere*):[13] that conduct should be in accordance with our profession. For St. Benedict passes a strict sentence upon those who call themselves monks but lead a worldly life and "lie to God by their tonsure."[14] *Hoc sit quod dicitur* [let it be what it is called].[15] These are the watchwords of our fathers: truth, simplicity in all things, *unity* as opposed to *duplicity*: our behavior, our name, our profession, all should be reducible to one and the same thing.

It is this spirit of truth that will enable the monk to produce a faithful copy of the model and exemplar cause of man: Jesus Christ, *imitans dominum.*[16] This is his way to God, the supreme Truth.

St. Bernard writes:

> "Come, saith the Lord.—Whither? Unto me, who am truth. . . ."[17]

"O truth, homeland of the exile, and his exile's end!" *O Veritas, exulum patria, exilii finis.*[18]

Our fathers, then, prided themselves on their desire to have their whole order become as it were, obsessed with the holy Rule. Short as the *Little Exordium* is, it contains twenty-four allusions to the Rule. They maintained that they would not come to any decisions except when the light of St. Benedict's spirit showed them the way. Let us listen with veneration to these words of St. Stephen: "They cast aside everything else that did not accord with the *purity of the Rule*. And as they took the whole Rule, just as it stands, and made it the *yardstick by which they measured their entire lives*, they conformed themselves to it, step by step in all observances, whether ecclesiastical or otherwise. Thus they were able to rejoice," the *Exordium* continues, "in having put off the old man and clothed themselves in the new."[19]

Puritate Regulae, the purity of the Rule! The expression is full of the savor of genuine simplicity, and what follows serves only to bring out its import with still greater clarity: *sicque rectitudinem Regulae supra cunctum vitae suae tenorem ducentes* [so that, directing the whole course of their life by the Rule over the entire tenor of their life]. These lines clearly prove that if one were to look upon the exodus from Molesme as a matter of external observances and nothing more, he would have failed to grasp the meaning of that great event, the principal reason for which was, in actual fact, the desire to return to the integral spirit of St. Benedict.

The last words of the passage, *novum hominem se induisse gaudebant* ["they were rejoicing to have put on the new man"], reveal to us all the joy of living there is in the spirituality of St. Benedict, which is so entirely simple because it is centered on the desire to "put on Jesus Christ." The soul of the monk is to reproduce the inner life of his master by observing this Rule. That is all.

As a matter of fact, the more we contemplate the character of the Savior in its majestic and supremely appealing serenity, the more we realize that his human nature can be summed up in the simplicity with which it portrayed his divine nature. *Deus vere et summe simplex est* ["God is truly and supremely simple"],[20] says St. Augustine. The entire life of the Incarnate Word manifests the essential and uncommunicable perfection of the Godhead: simplicity.

The Holy Ghost showed St. Benedict that the service of Christ could be expressed in terms of a practical plan of action in the words: *"Your life is hidden with Christ in God"* (Col 3:3)[21] and completed by the following: *"Let us share in the passion of Christ by our own patience."*[22] We imitate Christ's aversion from the spirit of the world, and his union with his Father, as manifested by his thirst for the solitude and silence that would enable him to spend hours at prayer. We imitate Christ in his spirit of humility and renunciation, inspired by the privations and destitution of his whole life. St. Benedict's entire doctrine is nothing but the imitation of the Savior's simplicity of outlook, by which he was led to discard everything that did not lead to his Father. This is indeed the ideal that St. Benedict brought before the world when he wrote his Rule, and that Rule is a miracle of discretion because it is a masterpiece of simplicity.

Like all other great men, who were great either because of their virtues or of their genius in science or in government, the patriarch of Monte Cassino reflects a few rays of the infinite simplicity of God.

Like them, he had a very clear and therefore a very simple view of a great end, and of the most efficacious means for

attaining it: and, like them, he not only cast aside everything
that had nothing to do with his ideal, union with God, but
he even refused to be encumbered with secondary or merely
indirect means of getting what he desired. St. Benedict was
guided by the spirit of simplicity,[23] and therefore he would
have souls unify their plan of sanctification, and simplify all
their means to that end. And how simple he is when he comes
to work out his spirituality in those observances by which he
seeks to express the simplicity of the Gospel: the doctrine that
"one thing is necessary," *unum est necessarium*.

What he was aiming at was harmony between the
demands of grace and those of nature. He is careful not to
crush the latter, but he keeps his eye on its slightest vagaries. If
he prescribes his *dura et aspera* ["hardships and difficulties"][24] in
the form of long prayers, obedience and the common life, fasts,
abstinence, vigils, manual labor, and, above all, *separation from
the world*, it is only in order to forestall and punish these vagaries according to the measure demanded by the end in view.

Since it was only in very exceptional cases that the monk
would be called to the external ministry, St. Benedict insisted
that enclosure should be rigorously observed, and that his
religious avoid everything that might militate against a life of
recollection, such as worldly contacts, traveling outside the
monastery, receiving visitors, idle conversations and letter
writing, recreation, and so on. All such things are considered
as an obstacle to the real vocation of a cenobite, to *"put on Jesus
Christ."*

But the holy patriarch views external observances only in
relation to the ideal of union with God. Spiritual reading and
prayer are there to surround these observances with an atmosphere of expansion and joy—joy that does not exclude holy
compunction, the peaceful and constant sorrow of repentance,
but which is, indeed, nourished by it.[25] Mental prayer and the
Divine Office are combined in a manner most harmonious
to the great benefit of both body and soul, and the result is a
unification and simplification of the entire life of the monk to

produce in him the habit of *breathing God* in deep and continuous draughts in all simplicity, and with the dispositions of a child. This produces in the soul of the monk a progressive formation of the Christ-life as it is lived in the Church, and plunges him into God with a solid and generous devotion.[26]

Nowhere in the spirituality of St. Benedict do we find anything that imposes a system upon the inner life of souls or brings them into dependence upon a method. The monk in his cloister has the constant development of the spirit of adoration, of reverential fear, of confidence and love in the simultaneous interplay of psalmody, mental prayer, and self-custody, and all this creates an atmosphere of luminous, warm, and strong vitality which is far superior to any method.[27]

Such is the great and *tremendously simple* spirituality of monasticism and it has power to inspire the strongest of loves and, hence, the most uncompromising renunciation.

Such also is the ideal of our Cistercian fathers: *To keep the Rule in all its purity* in order to *put on Jesus Christ* and arrive at union with God. Judging all things in the light of this end, they reject all excess, and every superfluity that might retard their progress. Simplicity of outlook leads to simplicity of life. *Si oculus tuus fuerit simplex*, says our Lord, *totus corpus tuum lucidum erit*: If thine eye be single, thy whole body shall be lightsome (Mt 6:21, Lk 11:34).

In their task of returning to this "purity of the Rule," the founders of Cîteaux insisted, first of all, where observances were concerned, upon reestablishing all that is clearly laid down in the Rule, and then upon getting rid of everything that was definitely not in accord with its meaning.

On the other hand, when they came to consider points that were mere probabilities, as for example the prohibition of fowl in the monastic diet, they took good care not to declare *a priori*: "The letter of the Rule does not expressly forbid it, let us therefore take advantage of this silence and give the benefit of the doubt to nature." They chose, rather, to apply this principle:

St. Benedict could not foresee everything, but his zeal for humility, for poverty, and for frugality of life is so striking in many passages of the Rule and in many traits of his life, that we must faithfully presume his interdiction or limitation of this or that particular thing. For the rest, wherever there is doubt, we prefer to favor grace rather than nature.

Furthermore, one thing our fathers never forgot was this: although he came of patrician stock, St. Benedict desired his monks to follow the example of the Desert Fathers and base their diet, clothing, and labor upon the common practice of the farm laborers in the country around about them. Let them use whatever may be had at the cheapest price—"*quod villus comparari potest.*" Let them not worry about the quality of the cloth—"*de grossitudine non causentur monachi*"—but let them be satisfied with whatever can be obtained in their district—"*quales inveniri possunt in provincia qua degunt.*"

After this general survey, let us now consider the essential observances instituted in the *Little Exordium*, and which St. Stephen thought should be sanctioned by pontifical approbation—observances which were to be, for approximately two hundred and fifty years after the foundation of Cîteaux, the basis for all decisions of the General Chapters.

In the following words of the *Little Exordium* our fathers declared that nothing, not even what had reference to divine worship, escaped their vigilance on behalf of evangelical simplicity. *Tam in ecclesiasticis quam in caeteris observationibus Regulae vestigiis sunt adaequati seu conformati*: In liturgical and all other observances they closely followed the guidance of the Rule and conformed themselves to it.

1. St. Alberic and St. Stephen first of all turned their attention to everything relating to clothing, bedding, and diet. *Rejicientes a se quidquid Regulae refragabatur*—rejecting all that was contrary to the Rule.[28]

These words of the *Little Exordium* bring us face to face with the lines just quoted from the Rule, as well as with expressions like the following: *Quod supra fuerit superfluum est et amputari debet.* ["Whatever goes beyond this is superfluous, and is to be cut off."] *Sufficere credimus ad refectionem quotidianem tam sextae quam nonae omnibus mensis cocta duo.* ["We believe that two cooked portions will be quite sufficient for the daily meal, whether it be served at the sixth or the ninth hour."][29]

The terms *sufficere credimus* or others equivalent to them recur frequently under the pen of St. Benedict.

Hence our fathers, in the very beginning of the fifteenth chapter of the *Exordium*, repudiated all flowing robes, furs, underclothing, great capes, breeches, overcoats, or bedspreads, as well as all foods which went beyond the limits of the Rule in their quantity or in the care with which they were prepared. St. Bernard faithfully echoed the *Little Exordium* when, in chapters 9, 10, and 11 of his *Apologia* he inveighed vehemently against every violation of simplicity in the diet or clothing of monks.

2. Then, after that, simplicity in all sources of income was imposed upon the order. There was to be nothing in common with the great feudal lords, nothing that savored of ecclesiastical benefices. The monks were to support themselves in all the simplicity of the Holy Family at Nazareth, of the apostles, of St. Paul. They were to live on the products of their own manual labor: and that was all. The *Little Exordium* lays this down in no uncertain terms. *Monachus qui terras suas possidet et per se et per pecora sua laborando vivat.*[30] ["The monk, who owns land, and should live by labor, and by raising livestock."] Once again, it is a return to the holy Rule. *Tunc vere monachi sunt si in labore manuum suarum vivunt, sicut et Patres nostri et Apostoli.*[31] "Then only are they really monks, if they live by the work of their hands, like our fathers and the apostles." *Occupari debent in labore manuum . . .*[32] ["They are to be occupied in the labor of their hands . . ."] *Nullus excusetur a coquinae officio . . .*[33] ["No one is to be excused from his weekly turn as servant of the refectory . . ."].

At the time when Cîteaux was founded, most other monasteries were supported by parish churches and altars which belonged to them, as well as by tithes on crops, farms, and the income of mills or manorial bakeries, and the labor of serfs. Our fathers list each one of these sources of revenue as being prohibited to the Cistercians.

Besides that, in spite of the fact that many monasteries guaranteed themselves large offerings by allowing persons of fortune to be buried within their precincts, the *Little Exordium*, recalling the fact that St. Benedict allowed the burial of no outsider except his sister, suppressed this means of procuring endowments.

Authorities in medieval history have emphasized the fact that the early Cistercians started a real social and religious revolution in the name of the spirit of simplicity so dear to St. Benedict.[34]

A century later, St. Francis of Assisi was to give a yet stronger impulse to this revolution, in the name of evangelical poverty and simplicity.

And so the *Little Exordium* commanded that the monks of our order should live solely by manual labor and raising stock.

Nevertheless, in order to be able to raise adequate revenues and to carry out the duties of charity toward guests and the poor, and to carry out the Rule day and night (*plenarie die sive nocte praecepta Regulae posse servare*[35]) and, above all, in order that they might be able to devote their full attention to the Divine Office, the monks admitted lay brethren into their community, treating them in all things, in life and in death, like themselves. The assistance of the brothers, however, was never to dispense the monks from manual labor: *monachus laborando vivat* [the monk lives by his own work].

The *Little Exordium* is never narrow in its interpretation of the Rule, and it allows the monks to employ secular workmen. It specifies that they may own farmland outside the enclosure, provided it is far-distant from the haunts of men. They may own mills and fishponds, and even distant granges.[36]

3. The next thing was simplicity in the matter of enclosure and in the exclusion of women. St. Augustine says: "If you disentangle yourself from the affairs of the world, you will

become simple: but if you allow yourself to become mixed up in them, you will lose your simplicity." (Literally, you will become *double*, that is, your soul will be divided against itself by distractions and conflicting appetites, drawing you away from your one true end, God.)[37] There is, in the heart of the monk, a powerful urge to simplify everything in his relations with the outside world. Were this not the case, how could he remain faithful to the name he bears since, etymologically, it means "solitary"?

St. Stephen had recalled St. Benedict's prescription that monasteries should be built in places far from cities or towns, or even from small villages. And so, as soon as he was elected abbot of Cîteaux, our holy founder shut the door against the Duke of Burgundy and any other prince who might wish to hold his court at Cîteaux, thus laying himself open to reprisals which were capable of bringing the abbey into the depths of destitution.

Wherever distant granges were maintained, they had to be placed in the charge of lay brothers alone, *quia habitatio monachorum secumdum Regulam debet esse in claustro ipsorum*—"since, according to the Rule, the place for monks to live is in their cloister." It is still the *Little Exordium* speaking.[38]

4. Finally, simplicity in all that concerns the worship of God. The restrictions in this matter were not due to St. Stephen alone. St. Alberic had already drawn up some regulations on this subject, since his program of simplicity applied *tam in ecclesiasticis quam in caeteris observationibus.*

Simplicity in the vestments: Chasubles were to be made of linen or wool, not silk. There was to be in them no gold or silver thread. The albs and amices had to be of linen. Stoles and maniples might be silk, but without any gold or silver thread. Copes, dalmatics, and tunicles were forbidden, as well as curtains and carpets (*pallia*). Altar cloths were to be of linen, without any embroidery.

Simplicity in the sacred vessels: Chalices and the tubes through which the Precious Blood was received in Communion by the monks[39] could no longer be made of gold but silver or silver gilt were permitted. Crosses of gold and silver were forbidden: only painted wooden crucifixes were permitted. A single iron candlestick had to suffice.[40]

St. Stephen, who referred to himself as a lover of the Rule (*amator Regulae*), left us an explanation for these severe limitations; it was, "to clear out of God's house, in which they desired to serve. God night and day, everything that savored of superfluity and display, *or which might injure poverty, the guardian of all virtues, and one to which they had vowed themselves. . . ."*[41]

The form taken by poverty among the Cistercians is perfect simplicity. Our fathers demanded the utmost propriety in the divine services, but justly feared that pomp might rapidly lead to the loss of the spirit of poverty and humility and, therefore, of simplicity in the order.

It has sometimes been insinuated that our fathers went too far in their thirst for simplicity when drawing up their regulations. They were carried away by the desire to react against tendencies which they regarded as clearly opposed to the spirit of poverty. However, the most competent secular writers on the origins of our order have found no difficulty in understanding their desires. Are we then, the sons of Cîteaux, going to be less capable of understanding them in our turn? Let us quote d'Arbois de Jubainville for one: "The lights were of a simplicity that bordered on cheapness, *if the motives of humility that inspired such a choice were not taken into account."*

St. Benedict and the first Cistercians certainly knew how to appreciate liturgical symbolism, but maintained the character of monastic simplicity in their expression of that symbolism. They did so deliberately. All they wanted was *to form monks* and to lead them to union with God by the *only great, direct means*: means which are at the same time more sure of success and productive of a fuller expansion in souls of some depth.

It never would have occurred to them to change their way of doing things because laypersons happened to assist at their offices.[42] Our founders, faithful to the spirit of St. Benedict, left the parish priests, who could not use these great means, to fall back on the expedient of liturgical splendor calculated to make an impression (always more or less superficial in any case) by exercising an attraction on the senses of their flock.

Let us hear what St. Bernard has to say about elaborate buildings and showy vestments and altar furnishings: "We well know that they (the secular clergy) are debtors both to the wise and to the unwise, and that they must therefore make use of material ornaments to excite devotion in a carnal people upon whom the things of the spirit have little effect."[43]

May we be permitted to remark that later on, especially in the days of the decline, when abbots began to obtain the privilege of pontificalia, Cistercian churches were seen to resemble splendid cathedrals.[44]

History preserves, with respect, the memory of a demand addressed to the Sovereign Pontiff by two great monastic orders which, in a century when the thirst for honors was almost universal, begged the Holy See not to erect their monasteries into abbeys, and not to impose the use of pontificals upon them. They said that they feared the loss of the primitive spirit of simplicity in their communities.

The author of the *Great Exordium* gives us a significant detail about St. Stephen Harding's pastoral staff. "This true pastor," we read, "abhorred all kinds of display. The pastoral staff he was wont to use in processions gives us the most eloquent testimony to this fact. This staff, preserved in the sacristy at Cîteaux, where it is held in great veneration, seems scarcely to differ from the sticks which old men and infirm use to support themselves." The *Exordium* continues: "Such was the abbot who formed our blessed father St. Bernard to the religious life: such was the perfect master who deserved to have that most perfect disciple."[45]

Of course, the *Great Exordium* is far from having the authority of the *Little Exordium*. It was begun at Clairvaux, probably toward the end of St. Bernard's life, or a little after his death, and even though it displays an excessive readiness to

accept as authentic various events of a preternatural character,
it is nevertheless a very valuable source of information when
it confines itself to relating the usages of the early Cistercians,
or incidents that manifest their spirit.

Therefore this point about St. Stephen's pastoral staff may
be accepted without hesitation, and it is enough to show with
what moderation and simplicity the saint would have made
use of pontificals if that privilege had existed at the time.

It is true that many splendid chasubles and expensive cro-
ziers and chalices are pointed out as having belonged to St.
Bernard. Guignard, together with other authors, thinks that
our holy father merely consented to make use of these things
in places where he happened to stop on his journeys.[46] On the
other hand, the linen chasuble that was still preserved in the
eighteenth century is generally accepted as having been in the
habitual use of the saint.[47]

In any case, all the evidence of the *Apologia*[48] and the let-
ters and life of the saint leads us to believe that in his accord
with the simplicity of the founders of Cîteaux, and even in the
liturgical objects in his use at Clairvaux, St. Bernard remained,
all his life, the perfect disciple of St. Stephen.

There are a host of texts from the *Apologia*: let us confine
ourselves to this one. "Tell me, ye poor folk (if poor you really
be!) what is all that gold doing in your sanctuary? What is the
object of it all? Is it the compunction of sinners? Or is it, rather,
the admiration of those who come to see?"[49]

How our blessed father must have thanked God when, in
1131, he saw with what admiration Pope Innocent II beheld the
beautiful and austere simplicity of the church at Clairvaux, as
well as the recollection of his monks, and their faces shining
with happiness in spite of the austerity and poverty of their
life.[50]

The *Instituta* in the *Little Exordium* confine themselves to
the four points that have just been discussed. Although they
do not take up many pages, let us remember that they are what
give the Cistercian order its own special essence, and they set

our fathers' interpretation of the Rule as quite distinct from every other. Now all these rules without exception deal with monastic simplicity. It was in order to live them that our fathers left Molesme. We have already seen, above, that St. Stephen brought these laws into effect not only at the Abbey of Cîteaux but also by reason of their authorization by the Holy See, in all the houses of the order, as a return to that Spirit *cui Beatus Benedictus abbas servivit.*

We agree: the *Little Exordium* has nothing to say about simplicity in the construction and decoration of churches and other buildings. But St. Bernard completes its teaching in several places, especially in his *Apologia.* True to his Burgundian nature, he speaks with a note of irony in his voice: "I shall not mention the tremendous height of churches, and of their immoderate length, their vast width, their sumptuous decorations and curious paintings which cause those who are supposed to be praying to forget their devotion and crane their necks and turn their heads about so that I am reminded of the rites of the ancient Jews."[51]

May we be allowed, at this point, a short digression? We are going to quote a few experts in architecture to show that the simplicity of Cistercian building, far from being detrimental to beauty, always contributed to bring out qualities of grandeur and dignity which did much to raise souls to their Creator.

Montalembert, an expert on early Cistercian architecture, was visiting the abbey of Fontfroide under the guidance of the abbot, Dom John, of holy memory. After he had admired the cloister, he spent some three hours in enthusiastic contemplation of the simple and powerful majesty of the church. He was able to pick out the precise shade of difference between the ideal of the Poverello of Assisi and the form of poverty adopted by St. Benedict and Cîteaux.

Dom Jean used to tell how he heard the famous author exclaim enthusiastically: "Look at that wonderful balance of grandeur and simplicity, of beauty and austerity, dignity and elegance, purity of line and practicality, solidity and grace!

What proportion, what harmony!" He kept repeating over and over, "The whole place literally sings of St. Benedict and St. Bernard!" until finally Dom Jean begged him to tell what he meant by these outbursts. Montalembert replied that he believed God must have shown these saints that, if they were going to dwell all their lives in solitude, there to advance to union with him by a spiritual life and by the suppression of everything that was not indispensable to nature, the monks, as a group, would need to be kept in a state of constant expansiveness of soul. The only great means for producing this are spiritual reading—especially Holy Scripture, with prayer and the eucharistic life: but God inspired our fathers with a supplementary means in support of these. He showed them that it was much better to refrain from decorating their churches and cloisters with all the frippery of second-rate art, and to fall back entirely on the beautiful and ample simplicity of an art that was stripped of all useless embellishments.[52]

But then it was quite a different story when Dom Jean flung open the door from the cloister into the chapter room. "St. Bernard is dead!" cried the great historian. "All that decorated Gothic smells of the decadence of Cîteaux: it does not interest me in the least." In fact, he would not even step inside.[53]

Another famous architect, Viollet-le-Duc, said: "The beauty of twelfth-century architecture springs from purity of line and harmony of proportions." Enlart, in his book on the most beautiful Cistercian abbeys, is unstinting in his praise of the genius of simplicity which their architects possessed. Emile Male, of the French Academy, a competent authority on religious art, is just as forthright in his views: "The plan of the Cistercian church, as it is preserved, for instance, at Fontenay, is one of *extreme simplicity*. The *simplest* possible forms are chosen, and deliberately so. The exterior of the church is as *simple* as the ground plan. Within, they are austere, grave, and pure as Christianity itself. *Everything that might have no purpose but to please the eye is excluded*: no triforium, no tribunes, no paintings, no stained glass; but, on the other hand, solid vaults, impeccable construction, and a vivid sense of proportion."

Everything that has been said about the simplicity of the founders of Cîteaux, both interior and exterior, is something that is everywhere and forever being proclaimed aloud, as it were, by the churches of the golden age of our order. Anyone who is able to read the message of the buildings which our fathers have left us finds there something of their soul, a reflection of their whole ideal, and a salutary lesson left by them to those who wish to remain loyal to their spirit.

Like the architecture of antiquity, that of the twelfth-century Cistercians, as harmonious as it is simple, breathes balance and calm because it is nowhere disturbed by any waste-motion. Everything about it is functional. Not only the great lines, but the least details are subordinated to the whole and correlated with the simplicity of the end in view. Hence, the lines are straight and tranquil. And because the beauty of the whole is nothing more than the result of the perfect harmony of proportionate parts, the total result is one of grandiose austerity—yet it is never cold or forbidding. It is too expressive for that.

Calm peacefulness, solitude, silence, vigorous childlike faith, the spontaneous surge of love, never spoiled by contact with the world nor by the mania for argument and hair-splitting, and never complicated by systems of spirituality—all these things guaranteed the early Cistercians all the leeway and breathing space of simplicity, that they might give themselves all of a piece to God, and go straight to their ideal, an ideal as great as it was luminous. Their architecture had to express this outlook. Anything that failed to reflect their simplicity, everything that, by its lack of sobriety, and its purposelessness to them, might have come in conflict with their ideal, would have been simply inconceivable.

Unity, finality, sincerity, rectitude, purity, naturalness, nobility, sobriety, proportion . . . the old Cistercian churches were all that.

God grant that we may become capable of understanding and appreciating our *Cistercian aesthetics*, and that we may thus be proud to go to that source for inspiration not only in building future monasteries, but also in everything to do with the liturgy, and, *a fortiori* for the furnishings in other parts of the monastery.

The churches of Pontigny, Fontenay, Noirlac, Aiguebelle, Acey in France; Fountains in England; Orval and Villers in Belgium; Fossanova and Casamari in Italy; La Oliva and Poblet in Spain; Doberan, Heisterbach and Chorin in Germany;[54] and many others still are at least in their *original* portions, fine specimens of the architecture of the Cistercian golden age. We are justly proud of our twelfth-century Cistercian style, a Burgundian style which, purified in accordance with the austere tastes of St. Bernard, combines the round and pointed arch. Even in the thirteenth century, this style remained true to the Cistercian spirit, combining the noble, expansive, sure taste of the man of quality with the austere simplicity of a true monk.

The aim of this third chapter was to show that a jealous love of simplicity sums up the reasons why Cîteaux was founded. It is, therefore, quite correct to call that virtue a characteristic of our order. Since that is the case, would not a definite tendency to forsake it, on our part, stamp us as no true sons of the saints, our founders?

4

ANXIETY TO
PRESERVE
SIMPLICITY

A great zeal for simplicity is evident in the decisions of the first general chapters. St. Raynard, in issuing the first collection of such decisions, the *Instituta Generalis Capituli* (1134) lists the titles of the first ten and sums them up in the following words: "So far we have given the ordinances concerning the first monks of Cîteaux, and they are practically all taken from the Charter of Charity."[1] There is no better evidence than this, of the respect in which the capitular fathers held the Charter of Charity and the *Little Exordium* on which it rests. Nor is there any clearer indication of the program which engaged all the attention of the general chapters of those times, which was either to recall the erring to obedience to some point in either of these two documents or else to state more precisely how they were to be applied in particular cases under their jurisdiction.

In his preface, quoted above, Guignard brings out this close parallel by quoting a passage from one of the two sources alongside of each decision.

Practically every one of them shows how our fathers were obsessed with solicitude for the spirit of simplicity, and each time there is any sign of deviation from this distinctive trait of

our order, the chapter sternly summons the delinquent back
to conformity.

For instance, in chapter 20 of these *Instituta* we find the
extremely significant prohibition of all sculpture and painting,
even in churches. The reason is given: "When the attention is
diverted to such things, the fruit of a good meditation is often
lost, or else the recollected demeanor befitting a true religious
is no longer preserved."[2] Only painted crucifixes were allowed.

The second official collection of decisions of the general
chapters (promulgated in 1240 and 1256) and called *Institutiones Capituli Generalis* brings us to the end of the Cistercian
golden age. It lasted a century and a half.

Most remarkable during all this first period was the jealous defense of simplicity by the capitular fathers. They had
not forgotten that when St. Bernard received Innocent II at
Clairvaux, they had no wine of good vintage to offer him, and
he had to be content with vegetable soup. "They were barely
able to find a fish to serve to His Holiness, and the monks
enjoyed only the sight of it. And in this banquet," continues
Ernald, a contemporary of the saint, "turbot was replaced by
vegetables, and so was dessert." What is more, at the papal
banquet, the "bread still contained its bran."[3] For the rest, the
Institutiones Capituli Generalis declare that white bread, if any,
is to be reserved for the sick and for guests only.

These chapters were not so busy watching over the clothing, diet, and bedding of the monks, or manual labor and
enclosure, as in repressing the excessive development of farm-
lands, display in building and in liturgical ornaments, and
useless embellishments in the sacred chant. The Charter of
1214[4] forbade all further purchase of lands and domains. They
already shrank from the menace of wealth. When St. Stephen
had spoken of the extension of the domain of Cîteaux, he had
been able to add that "this took place without harm to the
religious spirit—*nec religione decrevit.*" Too often it was not so.

As for the liturgy, our order had already begun to give in to the influence of other orders, some decadent, others engaged in the apostolic life.

But the general chapters were on the watch, and were not slow to act. Here is a fact that tells us so: In 1157, the general chapter permitted church doors to be painted white. It was, therefore, necessary to obtain its authorization even for so small a thing as this!

A few more decisions: The Chapter of 1152 permits abbots to wear silk copes only at the ceremony of their blessing. The Chapter of 1182 orders the destruction of all stained glass windows. Only those that are without color, or at least without any elaborate design, may remain. The Chapter of 1207 specifies that chasubles are to be of one color only, with no gold embroideries or ornamentation. Only in 1226 would an exception be made for chasubles accepted as a gift.

The abbot of Clairvaux had to obtain the authorization of the General Chapter of 1220 before he could light a candle before the relics of St. Bernard. In 1235 the abbot of Le Gard was ordered to destroy the mosaic pavement of his church, since it was against the regulations laid down by the general chapter. In 1255 the abbot of Royaumont, who had put up an altar decorated with paintings, sculpture, hangings, and columns with angels on top of them, was ordered, in spite of the fact that his was a royal monastery,[5] to destroy the whole business within a month, under pain of being deprived, together with his prior, of wine. In 1240 the chapter suppressed all pictures on altars, while at the same time stating that it was permissible to paint the altars themselves as well as church doors. Even though at this chapter permission was granted for a second candle at the high altar, it was nonetheless specified that this was only to be on feasts of sermon. Besides this, the same chapter prohibited the burning of a wax candle on the altar of a saint, even on his feast day, allowing only the use of a lamp or a tallow candle.

All mural painting was still forbidden in our churches. As for sculpture and decorated pavements, the unshakable

desire to cling to the spirit of the first Cistercians is shown
by these words, used nearly at the end of the golden age, in
prohibiting "all superfluities and every notable form of show
in sculptures, buildings, pavements, and other such things,"
which are classed with "all that corrupts the ancient purity of
the order, and ill-suits our poverty."[6]

It was not until 1256 that the use of silk in the decoration
of altars was finally authorized.

The acts of the General Chapter of 1199 contain a characteristic detail which shows what care was taken in those times
to preserve simplicity in *intellectual pursuits*. Monks who were
afflicted with the mania for writing poetry were to be sent to
another house.[7]

To sum up: All through the golden age we can find nothing in the statutes of the general chapters that is in the least
opposed either to the spirit of the *Little Exordium* or to its letter.
And the author of an abridged history of the Cistercian order, a
monk of Thymadeuc, says in analyzing the *Institutions Capituli
Generalis* that "in spite of the abuses that tended to creep in, the
order wanted to remain faithful to the *poverty, simplicity, and
discipline of the early days*."[8]

Let us call the century following the hundred and fifty
years of the golden age, the silver age.[9] From the beginning
of this second period, the general chapters had to act with
greater frequency against abuses in the matter of clothing. The
Chapter of 1263 prohibited the wearing of fur coats even by
the sick, and formulated sanctions on that point. That of 1269
recommended the avoidance of singularity in articles of dress,
and especially prohibited the use of long, flowing cowls. This
prohibition was renewed in 1303, and all who wore garments
of excessive elegance were to be deprived of wine.

There is a certain element of humor for us in the lesson
in simplicity given by the following prescription against an
exaggerated care for personal appearance under the pretext of
cleanliness: During the first century of the order, our fathers
only shaved *seven times a year*. Gradually the number of shaves

increased. It rose to nine in 1191. At the end of the golden age, they still shaved only *once a month*. But thirty years later (1293) they were shaving every fortnight. At that time, the Dominicans, even though they were called upon to appear publically in the pulpit, were still content to shave at three-week intervals.[10]

An important event occurred in 1256 to alter the situation regarding liturgical ornaments. Pope Alexander IV wrote to the general chapter inviting the venerable assembly to show itself less severe in the use of certain liturgical vestments.[11] The Chapter of 1257 emphasized the fact that they were only acting under obedience to the Sovereign Pontiff: "At the request and on the advice of our most Holy Father the Pope, who has written to the General Chapter on this matter, it is decided that . . ."[12]

So, the chapter permitted abbots to wear the cope, but *only* when there was a procession, at which the crozier was carried and white vestments were worn, as well as at the blessing of novices. Dalmatics and tunics were also allowed to the sacred ministers, but only when the abbot officiated, or was expected to do so.

But the Chapter of 1258 feared that some might use this permission as an occasion to go too far astray from the spirit of simplicity, for, it said: "Innovations are rather to be restricted than extended." Hence, it hastened to prohibit copes, dalmatics, and tunics that might be decorated with ornaments "in any way affected, precious, or variegated, no matter how they may have been obtained." Is it not gratifying to see how, even a hundred and sixty years after the foundation of the order, instead of seizing upon the opportunity to rush headlong through the door that had been half opened by the Holy See, our fathers remained scrupulously faithful to the spirit of the *Little Exordium* and of St. Bernard?

As for new buildings, many a time the chapters had to recommend a strict watch over simplicity to the fathers immediate and all the visitors, both during the golden and the silver ages. To put a stop to certain abuses that were creeping in, the Chapter of 1157 forbade stone belfries, or even wooden belfries of too great a height, and the weight of bells was limited to five hundred pounds.

Even though the spirit of the *Little Exordium* was somewhat mitigated during the silver age, the general chapters nevertheless wished to maintain the spirit of Cistercian simplicity, and, in the face of certain abuses, they took an uncommonly energetic and clear position. But the age of gold had nevertheless passed, and although Pope Benedict XII, a former Cistercian monk of Fontfroide, intervened in 1335 to put a stop to ill-considered temporal enterprises, ensure regular visitations, curtail egress from the enclosure, and suppress all that was unnecessary in clothes, food, and dormitories, his celebrated bull *Parvus Fons* was almost without lasting effect.

Worse still, after the middle of the fourteenth century, a number of different causes combined to hasten the decline. The disease tightened its grip and if the general chapters were powerless to cure it, it was because they were only held at rare intervals, were ill-attended so that they could no longer keep an eye on disorders, and such sanctions as they adopted were never applied.

The Black Death, the incessant wars of the time, the *commendam* and, later, Protestantism, all contributed, of course, to speed the process of decay. But the chief thing was that the order was less and less prepared to defend itself against these external enemies and against the general environment of a Christianity that was worse than tepid. This helplessness was due, in large part, to the loss of the spirit of simplicity. What was left of the spirit of the Rule and of the *Little Exordium*? The simplicity of the Cistercian program had given in to the pressure of the pride of wealth. This pride brought with it a thirst for more and more land, a love of luxury and comfort, and, in consequence, the loss of the ideal of separation from the world which is so intimately connected with the spirit of simplicity.

There were a good number of abbots who cared little for the obligation to reside in their abbeys. They could no longer follow the development of souls, or offer them a good example. They were poorly qualified to form true monks, men who loved solitude because they loved Jesus of Nazareth, Jesus humble and poor and hidden, with such simplicity, through love, in the heart of his Father. These abbots got to the point where they were traveling around with all the pomp of ecclesiastical grandees or the temporal lords of the land.

The order passively absorbed the poisonous influence of a frivolous society, and indeed its members were often more anxious to achieve brilliance in the eyes of men than to enter upon the path of the evangelical counsels. *The simple interior life was no longer enough for monks: indeed, it was often merely a burden to them.*

Solitude, enclosure, silence, a humble, poor, and hidden life, manual labor—all these things held no attractions for decadent monks. Recollection and prayer tended to be replaced by splendid churches, magnificent ceremonies, a highly ornate form of chant. The time came when the houses and buildings in which monks lived became as comfortable and lavishly decorated as the homes of men of the world. They liked to have visitors: in fact, not only did they allow seculars to come and encumber their cloisters, but they even urged them to do so.

At a time when the number of vocations decreased, abbots tended to prefer quantity to quality. As for studies: if their sole object was to prepare a man for the interior life, and not to lead to a doctor's degree, they were not considered to be of much value.

And so when, after plagues, famines, wars, and the depredations following in their train, the wealth of the monasteries had melted away, monks were no longer able to bear the austerities of the order or the privations permitted by Providence: still less to taste the joys that these things bring with them.

We must, nevertheless, recognize that the General Chapter of 1493 adopted the measures proposed in the so-called

Articles of Paris, and that later on the Chapter of 1667 resolved
to apply the constitution of Alexander VII which aimed, among
other things, at restoring simplicity in the dormitories and
in clothing, the suppression of linen shirts, and the return to
abstinence. "The furnishings of the dormitory," said the pope,
"are to be in accordance with the poverty professed by monks,
and there shall be nothing superfluous about them. All, abbots
as well as monks, shall wear simple clothing, of no other colors
than black or white, so that there may be nothing about them
that savors of the fashions of the world."[13]

A few revivals of fervor which were, as a matter of fact,
prompted by the action of the Holy See or of the General
Chapter proved that the sacred fire still smoldered under the
ashes. God did not want the total ruin of the Cistercian order.
He raised up several reforms, like those of the Feuillants and
of Upper Germany in the sixteenth century, that of Orval in
1605 while, in 1615 Denis Largentier began, at Clairvaux, a
movement to return to the primitive Cistercian life which his
successors so energetically and constantly defended under the
title of the "Strict Observance." Later, in 1663, at La Trappe and
Sept-Fons two other reforms gave the austere spirit of simplicity of the *Little Exordium* the same place of honor it had once
held at the order's beginning. And so, at the very zenith of the
seventeenth century the Cistercian annalist Manrique was able
to proclaim, with the enthusiastic approval of the entire order,
that the *Little Exordium* was "a book of gold, small in bulk, but
great in weight and worth."[14]

When the revolution broke out, Divine Providence con-
fided to Dom Augustin de l'Estrange the task of keeping alive
the sacred flame in the face of almost incredible difficulties.

5

LET US DIE IN
OUR SIMPLICITY

When, in 1892, Leo XIII proposed the fusion of the various branches of the Cistercian Strict Observance into a single order, the superiors who came together at Rome at the pope's invitation took as the basis for an understanding whereby to arrive at union, the return to our primitive usages in so far as it was possible. There indeed is the source where we find the Cistercian life in its purity, and the principle of vitality and unity. "Our aim," says St. Stephen, "is to live in the union of one charity, one Rule, and one set of customs."[1]

Since that time, the desire to find out more and more about the work of our holy founders has grown from day to day. There is an increasing desire to know not only the primitive observances but Cistercian spirituality itself. With this in mind, one of our recent General Chapters[2] encouraged the reedition of works by writers belonging to the first centuries of the order. There is no doubt whatever that the results of such work will be a composite picture showing how closely the simplicity of the gospels is followed by the observances of our fathers, because they are, in turn, so close to the ideal of St. Benedict.

St. Bernard, the most admired of our ascetic writers, is also, it would seem, *the simplest*. He, even more than any of the others, displayed, in his addresses to his monks, a single ambition: to follow St. Benedict for whom, as is so strikingly brought home to us by his sermon on the feast of our holy legislator, he cherished an admiration and love as deep as they were filial.

And St. Bernard gave these addresses in chapter after Prime, at which time, in accordance with what was prescribed by the Council of Aix-la-Chapelle at the behest of St. Benedict of Aniane, the superior was bound to explain the holy Rule, *etiam in Parasceve* [even on Good Friday].

Brilliant as the talent was with which the saintly abbot of Clairvaux *cast new light* upon the work of his beloved father, he does not step out of the role of a splendid commentator on the thought of St. Benedict when he (as he often does) praises the sublime greatness of the Incarnate Word concealed in the two words: *humiliavit semetipsum* [he humbled himself]. The energy with which he proves that the imitation of the poverty of Christ is the glory of the monk is further evidence of the same thing. His doctrine on humility, the "foundation," as he says, "and the guardian of all the virtues," and the harmony he established between humility and simplicity echo and amplify the meaningful words of St. Cyril: "There is no virtue more necessary to all men than modest *simplicity*."[3]

Has anyone ever shown more clearly than did St. Bernard the close connection between the two texts of our glorious patriarch: "The hard and repugnant things by which we go to God,"[4] and "let each one make his offering in the joy of the Holy Spirit"?[5] Who was ever more forceful in teaching his monks to understand, in this light, the deeply significant words of the Prince of the Apostles: "Rejoice in that you have a part in the sufferings of Christ" (1 Pt 4:13).[6] And to carry, all the more joyously, their austere bundle of myrrh (*fasciculus myrrhae*) (Sg 1:16) for the fact that their hearts will thus be able the more readily to sing *dilectus meus mihi, et ego illi* (Sg 2:16).[7] Who has ever surpassed the power and sweetness with which our holy father showed that devotion to Our Lady and the practice of fraternal charity will lead us more rapidly and more joyously and withal, with more sureness and strength, to live by Jesus and him crucified? There we have the simplicity of love carried to the point of immolation.

St. Benedict thought it sufficient to indicate, in general terms, toward the end of the seventh chapter, the wonders produced in the soul of a monk who has lived the Gospel precept *abneget semetipsum* [let him deny himself] right up to the hilt. The holy abbot of Clairvaux—we might well call him *Illustrator regulae*, with all the fire of his genius and of his love, brought out the full splendor of this doctrine. He showed how the union of the Incarnate Word with the soul, or, according to his own expression, the "fruition of the Word," is the fulfillment of a life of renunciation because once all the obstacles have been removed, the Holy Spirit can act freely and beget Christ in the soul. And it is in this manner that we arrive at that *delectatio virtutum,* that consolation in the practice of virtues—a phrase borrowed from Cassian by St. Benedict, and tied up, by him, with the love of Christ.[8]

St. Bernard heard these various summons of St. Benedict, urging the monk to the love of God: *pro Dei amore, . . . propter eum qui dilexit nos, . . . non jam timore gehennae sed amore Christi . . .* [for the love of God, . . . because of him who so greatly loved us, . . . no longer out of fear of hell, but out of love for Christ], etc. And, filled with the strength of these words, he enkindles such a great blaze of love in the soul of the monk who is faithful in following his guidance that, for such a one, love becomes not only the final cause of his practice of renunciation but also the efficient cause, and therefore the true source of motive power in his advance toward voluntary abjection and the joyful acceptance of suffering. So, says the saint, he who is far advanced in charity is ardent in embracing the cross, *amplectitur ardenter.*[9]

Finally, there is no one who has done more than our holy father St. Bernard to glorify the observances of the Cistercian order for being inspired by love of the Rule and by the virtue of simplicity.

Our other Cistercian authors, and to St. Gertrude the Great belongs a notable place among them, do little more than develop one or another of the theses dear to the mellifluous doctor.

The logic of the spirit of simplicity takes us inexorably back to our source. As sons of Cîteaux, it is our desire to find out what was prescribed and practiced by our first fathers, and what was written by our ancient authors. And when we find out that, above all, they wanted to be true sons of St. Benedict, this same logic must lead us to study with a more passionate interest the Fathers of the Desert, since St. Benedict, at the end of his Rule, would have us go to their school, and to that of the Fathers of the Church. He, as a matter of fact, drew his inspiration from their teachings, which he adapted to the manners of the people of Western Europe.

St. John Climacus, one of the most celebrated masters of the monastic life in the Near East, who died in 605, sixty-two years after St. Benedict, in a sense sums up his admiration for his illustrious predecessors, the Desert Fathers, in a cry of enthusiastic wonder at their simplicity, which had inspired all the virtues of their interior as well as their exterior life. "O goodly, O blessed simplicity!" he cries, first of all, speaking of those who already possess a natural inclination or love or attraction for this virtue. The holy author then hastens on to praise in even more glowing terms that simplicity which is the result of an acquired virtue: "How much more blessed and more noble still is that simplicity which we substitute for our own malice, in the sweat of our brow and with manifold arduous works." *Acquired virtue* has a technical meaning that is not intended here, it seems to me. Rather "the simplicity that comes after constant effort to overcome the impediments to it."

The words which he then adds give us every right to state that there is a clear connection between the doctrine expressed in chapters 7 and 72 of our holy Rule, namely those on humility and on "the good zeal" on one hand and the virtue of simplicity on the other. "This virtuous simplicity," says St. John Climacus, "is the mother and nurse of a most profound humility and of a great meekness. . . . Never is simplicity to be found where there is not, at the same time, humility also."[10]

St. John Chrysostom praises this same humility, the fruit of simplicity, in the solitaries of his time, while holding them up as an example to the Christians of Antioch: "They humble themselves," he says, "and abase themselves in all things, in their garb, in their cells and employments, and consider humility as the general end to which everything else is subordinated. Everything that enkindles the flames of pride, like fine clothes, splendid dwellings, numerous servants—things which lead us, in spite of ourselves, in the paths of vanity, are rejected by them. . . . In their very works and occupations the solitaries tend to humility and stifle every movement of vainglory in themselves. For who can become proud by digging in the ground, or watering plants, or making wicker baskets, or other such things?"[11]

There can be no doubt that the more we are able to get back to our various sources: Cîteaux, St. Benedict, the Desert Fathers, the Fathers of the Church, the more will we discover things that will help us the better to appreciate and love and, hence, to practice the virtue of simplicity, even down to its slightest outward manifestation: for St. Basil would have it that even in our clothing and shoes "we ought to prefer coarseness to elegance, in order thus to express our spirit of humility."[12]

The General Chapters will continue to encourage us in this return to our sources. That of 1925 proved it by its decision that the forthcoming edition of the *Usages* should mention, in its preface, as *fundamental documents* not only the holy Rule and the Charter of Charity, but also the *Little Exordium.* It also demanded that a paragraph be inserted somewhere in the *Usages* to remind the reader that simplicity must continue to characterize our holy order, not only in the furnishings of our guest quarters and in the reception of guests, but also in the clothing, manual labor, and lodging of the monks, as well as in everything concerning the buildings and liturgical objects destined for the worship of God.

The reader will no doubt excuse our inability to resist the pleasure of once again quoting St. John Chrysostom's words in praise of the dwellings of the man who has voluntarily embraced poverty.

"His bed is not made of ivory, indeed: his dishes are neither of silver nor of any other precious material: everything is earthenware, or made of wood. But it is this very fact that is the glory of his house. *This contempt for external ornamentation allows the soul to give itself entirely to itself, and to devote all its attention to becoming beautiful and precious in the sight of God.*

"Labor to adorn your house by almsgiving, prayer, supplication, and vigils. Such are the ornaments that please the King we serve.

"When the houses of Christians are without outward ornamentation, those who dwell therein are a far more striking ornament by the holiness of their life."[13]

Speaking of the simplicity of solitaries in the matter of clothing, the holy doctor had said in another place: "You never see them wearing such clothes as have been invented by the effeminacy or vanity of men. They imitate the garb of the great men of ancient times, those angels dwelling upon our earth in visible form, and blessed fathers of all solitaries: Elias, Eliseus, and St. John the Baptist."[14]

Filii sanctorum sumus. We are the sons of saints! St. Bernard and the founders of Cîteaux will allow us to call ourselves sons of theirs to the extent that we show our readiness to imitate, out of love, the humility and poverty of our dear Savior by responding to the invitation now extended to us all by the General Chapter.

This humble obedience on our part will increase a hundredfold our power over the heart of Jesus in winning from him the blessings of heaven upon our order, our various native lands, our families, and our own selves.

More than that: it will make us truly effective collaborators of Holy Church in her task of glorifying God and saving the world.

As to the power that will be at the disposal, in this regard, of all who are truly resolved to live in the full simplicity of the Cistercian spirit, a spirit that is nothing but contemplation and austerity, let us listen to the words of the Sovereign Pontiff Pius XI, in a bull—therefore in a document addressed to the universal Church.

"Those," he says, "who devote themselves assiduously to the ministry of prayer and penance contribute far more to the development of the Church and to the salvation of mankind than those who, by their apostolic labors, till the field of the Lord."

MULTO PLUS
ad Ecclesiae incrementa et humani generis salutem
conferre eos qui assiduo
PRECUM MACERATIONUMQUE OFFICIO
funguntur
quam qui Dominicum agrum laborando excolunt.[15]

The monumental words of Pius XI give us an unimpeach-able testimonial of the high esteem in which our Holy Mother the Church holds the contemplative orders, and the capital importance which she acknowledges them to have.

This sentence from the bull *Umbratilem* deserves a place of honor on the walls of our guesthouses and of our cloisters. It will enlighten secular visitors on the importance of the monas-tic life in society and, above all, it will help us, for our own part, to love our exalted vocation more and more.

As a matter of fact, this charter of the contemplative life was really granted by the Sovereign Pontiff to our own holy order in particular: for in the brief *Monachorum Vita*, in which, a month later, he approved our constitutions, he referred back to this bull, and even repeated certain expressions used in it. "We have already spoken elsewhere of those religious whose function in the Church it is to acquit themselves zealously of the ministry of prayer and penance."[16]

In this bull, the pope congratulates true monks on the pas-sionate devotion with which they have clung to their solitude, to the point of remaining strangers not only to the cares of the world, but also to all external ministry: *ab omni exteriore ministerio alieni ac vacui,* "separated forever from the society of men, whom they labor to save by a hidden and silent apostolate, they remain in their solitude and never leave it."[17] Their purpose in this is to devote themselves exclusively to contemplation: *ut ad caelestia unice intenderent animum* by following the way of an austerely penitential life: *asperrimae paenitentiae viam.* Do not the words of the pope: *ut ad caelestia unice intenderent* [that they may devote themselves exclusively to the quest of heavenly things] urge us on to the practice of interior simplicity?

Nor did he forget to point out that exterior simplicity is also a sign of a fervent monk. "Their simplicity is their best recommendation." *Simplicitate commendantur.* And he adds at once, "and by a certain holy rusticity of life" (*sancta quadam rusticitate vitae*).[18]

These eulogies on the lips of the vicar of Christ are a most precious encouragement for us, but they are also a lesson and a fatherly invitation to us to let ourselves be ever more and more penetrated by the spirit of simplicity of our first fathers and of all the saints of our order, and to profit by such luminous and eloquent examples.

"And therefore we also," as the apostle St. Paul has said in his epistle to the Hebrews, "having so great a cloud of witnesses over our head, *laying aside every weight,* let us run with perseverance to the fight proposed to us, looking on Jesus, the author and finisher of our faith" (Heb 12:1–2).[19]

MORIAMUR IN SIMPLICITATE NOSTRA!

ILLUSTRATIONS

INTERIOR VIEW OF THE ROSETÓN,
ARMENTEIRA ABBEY, SPAIN

SIDE AISLE IN THE CHURCH OF
FONTENAY ABBEY, FRANCE

THE CHURCH, LE THORONET ABBEY,
FRANCE

LAY BROTHERS' DORMITORY,
CLAIRVAUX ABBEY, FRANCE

MAIN CHURCH ENTRANCE, FOUNTAINS
ABBEY, YORKSHIRE, ENGLAND

EAST CLOISTER, CHAPTER ROOM ENTRANCE,
LE THORONET ABBEY, FRANCE

EASTERN END OF THE CHURCH,
FONTENAY ABBEY, FRANCE

CLOISTER ARCHES, LAS HUELGAS ABBEY,
BURGOS, SPAIN

CLOISTER ARCH, LE THORONET ABBEY,
FRANCE

EASTERN EXTERIOR OF THE CHURCH,
SÉNANQUE ABBEY, FRANCE

FLAT CHEVET OF THE CHURCH,
NOIRLAC ABBEY, FRANCE

FLAT CHEVET OF THE CHURCH,
SILVACANE ABBEY, FRANCE

LOOKING WEST IN THE CHURCH, NOIRLAC
ABBEY, FRANCE

PLAN OF A TYPICAL CISTERCIAN ABBEY IN THE TWELFTH CENTURY

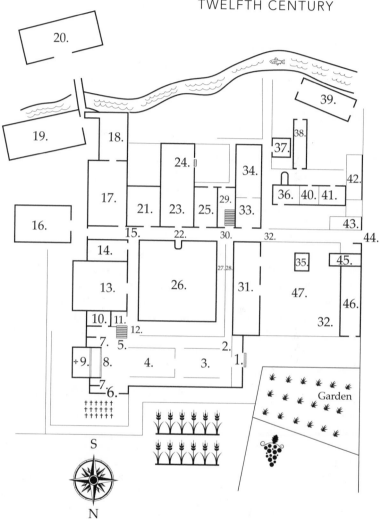

See Marcel Aubert, *L'Architecture Cistercienne en France*, especially volume 2 plan facing page 1. In Vacandard's *Vie de Saint Bernard*, vol. 1, there is a plan of Clairvaux in its fullest development, when it had expanded far beyond the limits of its original simplicity. This applies also to the plan in the *Compendium of the History of the Cistercian Order*, p. 122. It is based on Cîteaux at its highest point of development. The plan here given is based on twelfth-century Fontenay. Cf. *L'Abbaye de Fontenay*, by Lucien Bégule.

1. Entrance to the abbey church, and narthex (church porch)
2. Lay brothers' entrance to the church
3. Lay brothers' choir
4. Choir of the monks
5. The night stairs leading directly from the monks' dormitory into the church
6. Door leading from the church to the cemetery
7. Side chapels
8. Presbytery step (*gradus presbyterii*)
9. Altar step (*gradus altaris*) and high altar
10. Sacristy
11. *Armarium* or book room. Here the monks' collection of several hundred books were kept. Reading was done in the cloister. Big monastic libraries did not exist in Cistercian monasteries until after the twelfth century.
12. Monks' door to the church
13. Chapter room (*capitulum*). The abbot's seat was at the east end.
14. Auditorium (grand parlor). Speaking room, where work was distributed and where novices waited before receiving the habit. It served as the prior's office and if any talking had to be done it was done here.
15. Passageway
16. Infirmary, with its own chapel, etc.
17. Monks' workroom for indoor work, manuscript copying, etc. Not until the twelfth century did this room become a place for reading and writing for all the monks, corresponding to the modern monastic *scriptorium*.
18. Novitiate (*cella novitiorum*). The novices spent their time of probation segregated from the monks in this apartment reserved to them, but they assisted in choir with the rest of the community. Above the east wing of the monastery was the monks' dormitory.
19. Mill, forge, tannery, etc.
20. Barn
21. Heated room (*calefactorium*). This was usually the only room in the monastery, besides the kitchen, where there was a fire. The monks were not allowed in the kitchen except when they were serving their turn as cooks. But they could warm themselves in the *calefactorium*.
22. *Lavabo*, large fountain for washing, especially before entering the refectory for meals.

23. Monks' refectory
24. Reader's lectern, built into the wall, with its own window. The monks took turns reading to the brethren during meals. The reading was in Latin and aimed first of all at covering all the parts of scripture that were not read in church each year during the Divine Office. After that the writings of the fathers, etc., were read.
25. Community kitchen
26. Cloister garth [or préau; a courtyard in the middle of the cloister]. The cloister was the heart of the monastery. It was not merely a thoroughfare from one part of the building to the other. The monks lived in the cloister, gathered there for reading, etc.
27. West wing of the cloister
28. Lay brothers' passageway, separate from the cloister to which the brothers were only admitted on special occasions. They went to church through this passageway.
29. Cellarer's office. Here the cellarer, who had charge of all the material affairs of the monastery, did business with seculars, gave directions to the monks and lay brothers who worked under him, etc.
30. Stairway to lay brothers' dormitory. The lay brothers' dormitory was always in this wing of the monastery quadrangle.
31. *Cellarium*, storerooms for provisions, etc. This west wing of the monastery was the section where the material needs of the house were provided for.
32. Main entrance to the monastery
33. and 34. Lay brothers' refectory [with dormitory above]

Thus far, except for the buildings numbered 16, 19, and 20, the plan of the regular places was almost always exactly as they are presented here. This was the traditional and regular plan of all Cistercian monasteries in the twelfth century. In the hundreds of old monasteries that have been examined by scholars, only the smallest accidental variations are found in this fundamental plan. The biggest of these is that the church was often on the south side of the cloister instead of the north (for instance at Senanque) but it was always as nearly as possible "orientated" (with the high altar to the east) and the other regular places stood in about the same relative positions as they do in this plan. The buildings that follow were not so closely regulated and they could be placed wherever it was convenient. However, the workshops and other places of employment as well as stables and barns were often scattered around the main entrance to the monastery. The Cistercian monks made no pretense of presenting a decorated "front" to the outside world.

35. Winepress
36. Bakery and bake ovens
37. Shoemakers' and harness makers' shops
38. Stables
39. Cow barns
40. Workshop
41. Workshop
42. Infirmary for the poor
43. Porter's lodge
44. Main gate
45. Guesthouse chapel. The guests were usually not admitted to the offices in the abbey church.
46. Guesthouse. Visitors, pilgrims, and travelers were lodged at or near the gate. Their accommodations were never in the monastery itself.
47. Courtyard, or vegetable garden; also in the immediate vicinity of the monastery, within the enclosure would be found poultry yards, fishponds, orchards, vineyards, and so on. Outside the enclosure were fields of wheat etc., as well as woods, pastures, and quarries.

PART 2

ST. BERNARD OF CLAIRVAUX ON INTERIOR SIMPLICITY: TEXTS WITH COMMENTARY

THOMAS MERTON

INTRODUCTION

The Cistercian love of simplicity is more than a pious velleity that somehow crystallized into a system of spirituality bolstered up by arbitrary rules. On the contrary, the pages of the official report on the subject, to which the present pages serve as an appendix, have already shown us that Cistercian simplicity can be traced back to the very roots of Christian spirituality, in St. Benedict and the Fathers of the Church.

It remains for us to add a few extremely important quotations selected mostly from the sermons on the Canticle of Canticles, preached by the greatest doctor of Cistercian mysticism and spirituality, St. Bernard, to his monks at Clairvaux. These will do more than throw light on what has been said in the report: they will give us the massive dogmatic foundations upon which the Cistercian doctrine of simplicity is built as upon granite.

The whole aim of the Cistercian life—and the fathers of the order are unanimous on this point—is to set men apart from the world that their souls may be purified and led step by step to perfect union with God by the recovery of our lost likeness to him.

The fall and redemption of man, especially in their psychological aspects and implications, consequently become in the writings of St. Bernard matters of cardinal importance to which he frequently returns. It is in the finest sermons, the climax of his unfinished series on the Canticle of Canticles, that St. Bernard enters most deeply into this subject, as a preparation for the great discourses on the mystical marriage. And it is here that we find him introducing the topic of simplicity.

The soul was created in God's image and likeness. St. Bernard's whole treatment of the Fall can be summed up in this: that man lost his *likeness* to his Creator and Exemplar, but retained the *image*, ingrained in and inseparable from the very essence of his soul. To understand all that is implied by this is to possess the key to the whole mystical theology of St. Bernard and to hold the solution of all the problems which some may find in the apparent harshness of some of his early statements about humility. The whole tragedy of fallen man, from the point of view of his own spiritual condition, and the proximate cause of all unhappiness is the constant self-contradiction generated within him by the confronting of the essential *image* of God in his soul with the *lost likeness* that has been unutterably disfigured by sin.

Worse still in the soul of unregenerate man, slavery to sin, to pride and concupiscence only make this contradiction at once more horrible and more inescapable. In hell, the process goes on without end and with consequences that are unthinkable.

Now one of the ways in which St. Bernard, departing from the traditional Augustinian treatment of the subject, describes the divine image in the soul is to say that is consists in three things: man's natural *simplicity*, his natural *immortality*, and his inborn *freedom of will*. We shall see in a moment how the simplicity of man's soul, for which being and life, *esse* and *vivere*, are one and the same thing, stands halfway between the greater complexity of animal and vegetable creation, where matter lives by a principle other than itself, and the perfect simplicity of the Word for whom not only being and life are one, but life and happiness are also one and the same thing. For him, *esse* is the same as *beatum esse* [to be is the same as to be happy].

Now the true greatness of man consists (cf. Sermon 80 on the Canticle of Canticles) not only in his own essential simplicity, but in his ability *to rise to a participation* in the infinitely perfect simplicity of the Word. We too can share, by grace, that unity of *esse* and *beatum esse* which is his by nature. We too can be raised to such a state that to live will be perfect and unutterable delight, and life and joy will become in our souls the very same thing just as life and being are now one in them.

This greatness, of course, was not lost in the Fall. Without the redemption, this capacity would have remained forever unfulfilled, but it would have remained. What was lost was not the soul's greatness but its *rectitude*, its uprightness, its justice. To put it in other words, when Adam fell, he ceased to be *rectus*; he ceased to be *right*, that is, he ceased to be true to his own nature. He lost his *rectitudo*, and from then on it became impossible for him, without grace, to be true to himself, or true to the obediential potency for union with God which is according to St. Bernard the most glorious property of human nature.

God made us what we are, in his image. However, he did not make us *more* than this. The human soul is only made *ad imaginem, in* the image, a copy of the image. It is not *the Image* itself (*Imago*), for only the Word, the Second Person of the Holy Trinity, is that. Satan, however, tempted Eve to desire what man was not made to desire: divinity not *by participation* but independently of God's free gift, by our own right, by our own nature. It is in this sense that *eritis sicut dii* [you will be as gods] is to be taken. Eve was tempted to think human beings could become gods by natural right.

This pride was the birth of sin and the immediate ruin of our simplicity, involving as consequences our fall into servitude to sin and to death. How was our simplicity lost? Not by being destroyed. St. Bernard is always careful to insist that human nature was in no way harmed, in its essence, by the Fall. We always remain what God has made us in our essence, but the tragedy is that God's good work is overlaid by the evil work of our own wills. Hence our simplicity was not taken from us but, and this was far worse, it was concealed under the disfigurement of a duplicity, a hypocrisy, a living lie that was not and could not be natural to us or part of our nature, and yet which would inevitably cling to us as a kind of hideous second nature, but for the grace of God, who in his infinite mercy, sent his beloved Son to deliver us again by his death on the cross.

The following quotations have been selected to amplify St. Bernard's thoughts on our essential simplicity, and its corruption by the Fall. But they must be seen against their own proper background, the background of the Cistercian life. And the whole purpose of the Rule of St. Benedict and the Cistercian *Usages* is, according to St. Bernard, to keep man in an atmosphere where, by obedience, poverty, solitude, prayer, fasting, silence, manual labor, and the common life, he will be constantly running into occasions where he will be brought face to face with the truth about himself, and forced to recognize his misery without God, with the result that he will turn to God in supplication, begging him for that grace and infused charity which will enable him to purify his soul of the hideous layer of duplicity and free the divine image within him from all the sordid appetites and evil habits that cling so obstinately even to souls that have devoted themselves for years, with the most ardent generosity, to the wholehearted service of God in the cloister.

But this purification is only the beginning. As the Father looks down from heaven into the loving soul that seeks him in "tears of compunction" and beholds there the likeness to his Son reappearing, as the simplicity of the concealed image begins to be freed from the dark crust of sin, he instantly pours more love into the soul and raises it up toward him ever more and more, until finally, by a faithful correspondence to grace, the perfect image is restored, and the soul is now utterly purged of all the "fear" that is inseparable from "unlikeness" to God. From then on, the way to heaven is nothing but confidence and love, and St. Bernard does not hesitate to promise, as the *normal term* of the Cistercian life of simplicity, a perfect union of wills with God, by love, which he calls the mystical marriage.

OUR ORIGINAL SIMPLICITY

From Sermon 81 on the Canticle of Canticles, paragraph two:

Let the soul therefore realize that by virtue of her resemblance to God, there is present in her a natural simplicity in her very substance. This simplicity consists in the fact that for the soul it is the same thing to *be* as to *live*, but it is not, however, the same to *live* as to *live well*, or to *live happily*. For the soul is only like God, not equal to him. This is a degree of nearness to him, but it is only a degree.

For it is not an equal excellence or distinction to have an existence that is identical with life, and to have an existence that is identical with *happy* life. So, if the Word possesses this latter perfection, because of his sublime dignity, and the soul possesses the former by virtue of her likeness to him, without prejudice to his preeminence, it is easy to see the affinity of their natures; and it is equally easy to see the prerogative of the soul.

To make all this somewhat clearer, let us say that only for God is it the same to *be* as to *be happy*: and this is the highest and most pure simplicity. But the second is like unto this, namely that being and life should be identical. And this dignity belongs to the soul. And even though the soul belongs to this inferior degree, it can nevertheless ascend to the perfection of living well, or indeed of living in perfect happiness: not in the sense that being and happiness will ever become identical for her, even after she has completed the ascent.

Thus the rational soul may ever glory in her resemblance to the Divinity, but still there will also ever remain between them a gulf of disparity whence all her bones may cry out, "Lord, who is like unto thee?"[1] Still, that perfection which the soul possesses is great indeed: from it, and from it alone,[2] can the ascent to the blessed life be made.

Sermon 82.2–3:

The fact that scripture speaks of our present *unlikeness* to God does not mean that Holy Writ maintains the likeness has been destroyed, but that something different has been drawn over it, concealing it. Obviously, the soul has not cast off her original form, but has put on a new one foreign to her. The latter has been added, but the former is not lost, and although that which has been superinduced has managed to obscure the natural form, it has not been able to destroy it. "Their foolish heart was darkened," said St. Paul, and the prophet cried: "How has the gold become obscured and the finest color changed?" He laments that the gold has lost its brightness, and that the finest color has been obscured: but the gold is still gold, and the original base of color has not been wiped out. And so the simplicity of the soul remains truly unimpaired in its essence, but that is no longer able to be seen now that it is covered over by the duplicity of man's deceit, simulation, and hypocrisy.[3]

What a contradiction it is, this combination of simplicity and duplicity! How unworthy of the foundation is the structure we have erected upon it![4] This was the kind of duplicity the serpent put on when he pretended to be counselor and a friend in order to deceive. And his victims, the two dwellers in paradise, put on the same duplicity when they tried to conceal their now shameful nakedness in the shadows and foliage with garments of fig leaves and words of excuse. From that day forth how terrible has been the spread of that infection of hereditary hypocrisy throughout the whole race. Is it possible to find a single son of Adam who, I do not say is willing, but can even endure to be known for what he really is?

Yet nevertheless in every soul there still remains the natural simplicity of man together with the duplicity that came with original sin, *in order that these two contradictories*

*might persistently confront one another within us, to our own
greater confusion.* . . .

Add to this the fact that the desire for earthly things[5]
(all of which are destined to perish) increases the darkness
of the soul, so that in the soul that lives in such desires
nothing can be seen any more on any side, save the pallid
face and the image, as it were, of death. Why does not this
soul, since it is immortal, love the undying and eternal
things which are like itself that thus she might appear as
she truly is and live as she was made to live? But no, she
takes her delight in knowing[6] and seeking what is contrary
to her nature and, by living in this manner that is so far
beneath her, placing herself on the level of perishing things
and becoming like them, she blackens the whiteness of her
immortality with the pitch of this familiarity with death.[7]
For it is not to be wondered at that the desire of material
things makes an immortal soul like unto mortal beings,
and unlike to the immortal. "He that toucheth pitch," says
the wise man, "shall be defiled with it." The soul that seeks
to rest and take its fill of delight in mortal things[8] puts on
mortality like a garment, and yet the garment of immortality is not put off, but discolored by the arrival of this
likeness of death.

Consider Eve, and how her immortal soul overlaid the
glory of her own immortality with the shadow of death,
by giving her love to perishing things. For since she was
immortal why did she not despise mortal and transitory
things and remain satisfied with the things on her own
level, immortal and eternal? "The woman saw that the
tree was good to eat and fair to the eyes, and delightful
to behold." O woman! That sweetness, that beauty, that
delight do not belong to thee! Or if they do pertain to thee,
according to the portion of clay that is thine, they are not
thine alone, but are common to thee and to all the animals
on the earth.[9]

That which is thine, and really thine, is not to be found
here: it is something totally different from these: for it is
eternal, and of eternity. Why do you force your soul to take
on the impress of an alien form, or rather an alien deformity? Yea, indeed, that which she loves to possess, she fears
to lose. Now fear is a kind of color. It stains our liberty and,

discoloring it, conceals it, and, at the same time, makes it unlike to itself.[10] How much more worthy of her origin would it have been if only this soul had desired nothing, feared nothing, and thereby had defended its own liberty, remaining in her native strength and beauty![11]

Alas, she did not do so! The finest color is dimmed. Thou fliest away, Eve, and hearing the voice of the Lord thy God, thou hidest thyself! Why so, if not that him who thou once didst love thou now fearest and the form of a slave has superseded that of a freeborn child.

. . . Therefore, because man neglected to defend the nobility of his nature by leading an upright life, it has come about that by the just judgment of his maker he has not been stripped of his liberty but has been "clothed over with his confusion as with a double cloak" (Ps 108:29).[12] And the expression "as with a double cloak" is very apt, for now in the soul of man there are found both the liberty which remains because it is essential to his will, and his servile manner of life which is proof of his servitude. The same thing is to be observed in the case of the soul's simplicity and immortality. In fact, if you consider our present state well, you will see that *there is nothing in the soul that is not in the same way reduplicated—likeness to God being covered over with unlikeness.* Is it not indeed "doubled," this cloak, in which guile, which is no part of our original nature, has been sewed on to our simplicity, death stitched upon our immortality, necessity upon our liberty, and all by the needle of sin? For duplicity of heart does not exclude simplicity of essence, nor is our natural immortality destroyed by death, whether the voluntary death of sin or the involuntary death of the body. And the freedom of the will, likewise, is still there, underneath the servitude to sin.

And thus accidental evils superadded to the good that is in our nature do not suppress that good but are impressed upon it, defile it without destroying it, and lead to its upheaval, not its total removal. This is the reason why the soul is unlike to God, and why *it is even unlike itself.* This is the reason why it "is compared to senseless beasts and is become like to them."[13]

Practical Application of This Doctrine of St. Bernard

Even a cursory reading of these notions, which are the very cornerstone of Cistercian asceticism, will show that St. Bernard has really vindicated the fundamental goodness of human nature in terms as strong as have ever been used by any philosopher or theologian. And if the first step in the Cistercian ascent to God is for the monk to *know himself,*[14] we may reasonably say that, in some sense, the whole life of such a one will consist in *being himself,* or rather trying to return to the original simplicity, immortality, and freedom which constitute his real self, in the image of God.

We will never completely succeed in being ourselves until we get to heaven. Meanwhile on earth our chief, in fact our only, task is to get rid of the "double" garment, the overlying layer of duplicity that is *not* ourselves. Hence the Cistercian stress on simplicity. Hence the fact that the whole of Cistercian asceticism may be summed up in that one word.

And this is true even when the word is taken in several different senses.

1. The first step in the monk's ascent to God will be to recognize the truth about himself—and face the fact of his own duplicity. That means *simplicity in the sense of sincerity,* a frank awareness of one's own shortcomings.

2. He will also have to overcome the temptation to excuse himself and argue that he is not, in fact, what he is (whether he argues with other men, with himself, or with God, it does not matter.) Hence *simplicity in the sense of meekness—self-effacement, HUMILITY.*

3. He must strive to rid himself of everything that is useless, unnecessary to his one big end: the recovery of the divine image, and union with God. Now, simplicity takes on the sense of total and uncompromising *mortification.* (a) *Of the lower appetites*: hence the simplicity in food, clothing, dwellings, labor, manner of life as laid down in the *Little Exordium, Consuetudines, Statutes of the General Chapters, etc.* This was covered in part 1, the official report to the General Chapter. (b) *Of the*

interior senses and the intellect: This means simplicity in devotions, studies, methods of prayer, etc., and calls for the complete simplification in liturgical matters and the decoration of churches for which the early Cistercians were so famous. (c) *Of the WILL*: This is the most important task of all. In the works of St. Bernard the amount of space devoted to other forms of mortification is practically insignificant in comparison to the scores of pages which are given up to the attack on self-will and its utter destruction. Hence the stress on the great Benedictine means of penance, which resumes all others for the monk: OBEDIENCE. This will produce that simplicity which is *synonymous with docility, the trustful obedience of a child toward his father. The supernatural, joyous obedience of the monk who seeks to prove his love for Christ by seeing him in his representative, the abbot.* See the next text.

INTELLECTUAL SIMPLICITY: HUMILITY IS TRUTH

Culpable ignorance: There are two kinds of knowledge which all men are bound to have, and the lack of which will result in their damnation: *knowledge of themselves* and *knowledge of God*.

From Sermon 35 on the Canticle of Canticles:

> Man, when he was in honor, did not understand (Ps 48:13). What did he not understand? The psalmist does not tell us: but we shall say what it was. Man, being placed in a position of honor (in paradise) failed to understand that he was slime, and that *he had been elevated* to this culminating dignity: and therefore he soon found out, in himself, that which many years later a man, a son of his captivity, also discovered and acknowledged in all truth saying: He who thinks he is something, when he is nothing, deceiveth himself (Gal 6:3). And thus a creature that was above the run of other animals has been reduced to the same level as the rest of the herd;[1] thus it is that the likeness of God has been changed into the likeness of a beast,[2] and thus it is, too, that man has exchanged the company of the angels for the company of the beasts of the field. *You see, then, how much we ought to avoid this ignorance which was the cause of so many thousands of evils to our humankind.*[3] For the prophet

says that the very reason why man was made like to the beasts of the field was that *he did not understand.*

But there is a second ignorance, even worse than the first. The first made us equal to the beasts, *this second places us below them.* It is the ignorance of *God* (Sermon 35.7).
Also from Sermon 35:

> He [the Wise Man] now shows us that there is a second ignorance which is far more to be feared, far more shameful than the first, for while the former made man equal to the beasts, this places him below them. For men deserve, by their ignorance, to be ignored, that is damned, by God, and to stand before his terrible judgment seat and to be cast into everlasting fire. None of these things will happen to the brute beasts.

Thus, the first reason why men are placed lower than beasts by their own ignorance is the fact that they must go to hell. But even in this life they are lower in another way.

> Do you not think that a man, born with reason, yet not living according to his reason, is in a certain way more of a beast than the beasts themselves? For the beast, who does not rule himself by reason, has an excuse in his very nature: since this gift is denied him by nature. But man has no excuse, since reason has been given him by a special prerogative. . . . Thus he is doomed to follow *after* the flocks of the other animals in this life because he has depraved his own nature, and in the next by reason of his extremely great punishment.

Why must we have this knowledge of God and of ourselves? For the sake of knowing? No, but in order to love God. We cannot love God unless we know him, and our love for him cannot be properly ordered unless it befits our state and condition in his sight: i.e., unless it is rooted in a deep sense of our misery and of our need for his mercy (Sermon 37.1).

> Self-knowledge is the mother of salvation, and of this mother is born humility, and the *fear of the Lord* which,

just as it is the beginning of wisdom, is the beginning of salvation.

. . . And what if you should fail to know God? How can there be any *hope of salvation*[4] where there is ignorance of God? It is impossible. *For you can neither love One Whom you do not know, nor possess One Whom you have not loved.* Know yourself, then, that you may fear God; know God, that you may also love him. Knowledge of yourself will be the beginning of wisdom, knowledge of God will be the completion, the perfection of wisdom; because the fear of the Lord is the beginning of wisdom and the fulfillment of the Law is *charity* (Rom 13:10).[5] Beware, then, both of ignorance of yourself and ignorance of God since there is no salvation without the fear and the love of God. *All other knowledge is indifferent, since the possession of it does not give us salvation, and the lack of it will never cause us to be damned.*

From Sermon 37:

But just as the beginning of wisdom is fear of the Lord, so the beginning of all sin is pride: and just as the love of God is the perfection of wisdom, so despair is the ultimate consummation of all malice. And just as knowledge of ourselves begets fear of God, and knowledge of God begets love of God, so on the other hand, from ignorance of ourselves comes pride and from ignorance of God, despair. . . . And pride, the beginning of all sin, consists in this: that you become greater in your own eyes than you are before God, than you are in truth. . . .[6]

From Sermon 38:

But in what manner does ignorance of God beget despair? Let us suppose that someone enters into himself, and is filled with sorrow for all the evil he has done, thinking to amend his life and to turn back from his evil road, and from his carnal ways: if he does not know how good God is, how gentle and how kind, how quick to pardon: surely his carnal thoughts will rebuke him saying: . . . Your sins are too great . . . you will never be able to make satisfaction for them. Your health is weak, you have led an easy life, you will find it terribly hard to break your old habits. These thoughts, and others like them, drive back into despair the unfortunate man who does not realize with what great ease the omnipotent Goodness Who is God would do away with all these obstacles.

From Sermon 36:

> Perhaps I seem to disparage speculative sciences and, as it were, to criticize learned men.[7] Far from it. I am well aware how much good has been and is done in the Church by learned men, both in refuting the errors of her enemies, and in instructing the unlearned.[8] Indeed, I have read in Holy Scripture: "Because thou hast refused knowledge, I will also refuse thee, and thou shalt not serve before Me as priest" (Hos 4:6).[9] And also: "Whosoever shall be learned shall shine like the splendor of the firmament; and those who have instructed many in justice shall shine like stars for everlasting eternity" (Dn 12:3).[10] But I also know where I may read that "Science puffeth up" (1 Cor 8:1).[11] And again, "Bring in knowledge, and you bring in sorrow."[12] So you see that there are different kinds of science, when one puffeth up, and the other makes sorrowful. Now I would have you tell me: which of these kinds of knowledge seems to you more useful, more necessary for salvation: that which puffeth up or that which causes pain? I do not doubt for a moment that you will prefer the science that fills you with sorrow to that which fills you with wind. The inflation of pride may make you feel healthy: but the sorrow of compunction will make you beg for real health instead of the illusory health of pride. But whoever begs for salvation is getting close to it already, because everyone who asks shall receive.

Remarks

1. St. Bernard applies the fundamental principle of simplicity to our intellectual life. The principle is to eliminate all that is superfluous, unnecessary, indirect, and to put in the place of these an exclusive concern with the *one thing necessary*—the knowledge and love of God, union with him, in the closest possible way. To simplify our understanding we abandon the knowledge of all that does not lead us more or less directly to

God. In St. Bernard's terms, since we cannot have any immediate knowledge of God in this life, we must at least seek that
knowledge which fills us with love of God: for our love can
attain immediately to him even on earth. Hence, simplicity in
the intellectual order means subordinating all our knowledge
to the LOVE OF GOD. We study in order to love. But it is by
loving that we really begin to know God as he is in himself, not
that love gives us new intellectual concepts of his essence or
his perfections but nevertheless it endows us with an intimate
experimental knowledge of God as he is in himself, by virtue
of the immediate contact which it establishes with him.[13]

This is clear from a typical passage in St. Bernard. In the
fifth book of the *De Consideratione*, having asked repeatedly
"Who is God?" *"Quis est Deus?"* and attempted to answer
the question by the most lofty intellectual speculations on the
Divine Essence, the saint concludes:[14]

> We know these things. But because we know them, do we
> imagine we have comprehended (*comprehendisse*) them?
> Philosophic argumentation can never comprehend them,
> that is a thing which sanctity alone can do if, indeed, they
> can be grasped at all. *Non ea disputatio comprehendit sed sanc-*
> *titas.* And yet unless it were possible, the Apostle would
> never have said *"in order that you may be able to comprehend*
> *with all the saints"* (Eph 3:18).
>
> Therefore the saints comprehend them. You ask how?
> If you are a saint, you comprehend, and you know; and if
> you are not a saint, then become one, and you will find out
> by experience. But it is a holy affection that will make you
> a saint[15] and that affection is twofold: the holy fear of God
> and his holy love. The soul that is altogether possessed of
> these two affections has, as it were, two arms with which
> it lays hold upon God and embraces him and hugs him to
> herself and holds him saying: "I held him and I will not
> let him go" (Sg 3:4).

These words of the saint recall what he has just been saying about the one kind of knowledge that is necessary. That
knowledge also was twofold: on the one hand it was necessary

for us to know ourselves, in order to fear God, and on the other, to know God in order to love him. Therefore, that knowledge endows us with the means of arriving at an experimental knowledge of God by direct contact with him. The knowledge itself does not enlighten our minds concerning him, but it leads to love and love gives us a concrete experience of God that tells us more about him than all the most sublime speculations of the theologians could ever do.

2. Therefore, it would be far from the truth to say that St. Bernard would have the monk renounce all knowledge and enclose himself in a kind of holy blindness and stupidity, making himself impervious to all truths and renouncing all books and all thought whatever. There is a certain holy ignorance which is incumbent on the saint: but this *docta ignorantia* is the ignorance of the things that are *useless* to him. And therefore, it is really a higher perfection of the mind, it is *docta*, "learned." It is more enlightened than the wisdom and prudence of this world, because it has renounced all the vain learning which only blinds the soul to higher truths and makes it incapable of the love of God.

St. Bernard, therefore, teaches that there is a twofold obligation for the contemplative monk: he is obliged to know the things necessary for his state, and he is obliged to renounce all useless learning that would only stand in the way of his vocation.

Therefore when Pope Pius XI was drawing up a letter to the heads of all the religious orders in the Church, to remind them of the necessity of a thorough philosophical and theological training for all religious priests, he most aptly quoted the very text from St. Bernard which we are commenting. At the same time, the holy father recommended St. Bernard, together with St. Bonaventure and St. Alphonsus Liguori as the most valuable masters of the spiritual life to whom religious ought to turn for guidance from the very first days of their vocation.[16]

In the sixty-ninth sermon on the Canticle of Canticles, St. Bernard again speaks of this harmony between knowledge and love, and stresses the obligation of both: the need of a knowledge that is enlightened but humble, and the need of a love that is aware of the great love of God for us and free to respond to it—not impeded, that is, by self-love and pride. *Non decet Sponsam Verbi esse stultam porro elatam Pater non sustinet.* "The Spouse of the Word," he says, "must not be stupid: but if she be proud, the Father will not be able to stand her."[17] Let us consider more closely the two members of this statement.

Non decet Sponsam Verbi esse stultam

The soul of the contemplative monk—the souls of all rational beings, too, for that matter—is called to be the Spouse of the Divine Word. But the Word is the uncreated Wisdom of God, infinite wisdom communicated to the soul. He himself comes to teach her, to communicate to her his own substantial, uncreated truth. Is the soul that is destined to become the bride of uncreated truth to live in union with him as a fool? The thought is blasphemy.

But St. Paul teaches us that "the wisdom of this world is foolishness with God" (1 Cor 3:19) and he also says that the learned men of the world "professing themselves to be wise, have become fools" (Rom 1:22).

Therefore when St. Bernard says that the Spouse of the Word must not be a fool, he clearly means that she must not be guilty of the egregious folly of presenting herself for union with the uncreated wisdom of God, clothed in the darkness and ignorance which earthly wisdom is in the sight of God.[18]

When we come to ask what is the wisdom of this world, we find that it consists not in a certain *type of subject matter* so much as a certain manner of knowing. The knowledge of created things is not reprehensible: far from it; we know that God made them precisely in order that we might use them to arrive at the knowledge and love of him.[19]

And yet there is a certain manner of knowing not only creatures, but even God himself, a vain, self-centered, empty form of speculation which is true as far as it goes, but is useless to us because it does not end in the love of God. And hence its truth is incomplete. Because if we really knew God, we could not help but love him. But God himself is truth. Therefore, any knowledge of any "truth" that does not directly or indirectly lead to the love of God is incomplete. If we possessed his truth, our possession would be manifested by our *love*.

In the eighth sermon on the Canticle of Canticles St. Bernard develops at some length the distinction between false knowledge, the "science that puffeth up," the "wisdom of this world," and knowledge of God by love. It is a distinction that had been long before set forth by St. Paul. The apostle said of the pagan philosophers that "When they knew God, *they have not glorified him as God, or given thanks*: but became vain in their thoughts, and their foolish heart was darkened" (Rom 1:21).

St. Bernard comments:[20]

> [T]hese pagan thinkers . . . being satisfied with the knowledge that puffeth up, never arrived at the possession of that knowledge by charity that edifieth . . . and it is evident that they did not really know God if they did not love him. For if they had known him completely, they would have known that goodness of his which willed to be born in human flesh, and die for their redemption.[21]

Then the saint continues: "Behold, these men pried into all there is of sublimity and majesty of God, prompted not by the Spirit of God but by the presumption of their own spirit: but they never understood that he was meek and humble of heart."

The great contemplative, who knew the immense goodness of God by mystical experience, could not help but be overwhelmed at this spectacle of a selfish and self-complacent knowledge that used its gifts to adorn itself with grand and empty conceptions, at the expense of God himself: exploiting, as it were, the perfections of their own creator, *not in order to admire him, but in order to admire their own wisdom*. Hence it was inevitable that they should be blinded, and that their pride should place an insurmountable obstacle between them and the truth who is God and who is, at the same time, infinitely pure love.

That brings us to the second half of St. Bernard's sentence:

Animam elatam Pater non sustinet

We possess the truth by a union of likeness with him. But what likeness is there between light and darkness, between infinite unselfishness and the narrowness of an almost infinitely petty pride? *Quid conventio luci ad tenebras?*

This kind of knowledge that instead of giving us the possession of truth bars us forever from that possession goes, in St. Bernard, by the technical name of *curiositas*—a term which the English "curiosity" does not quite express. But the concept has already been adequately described. *Curiositas* is that vain and illusory knowledge which is really ignorance, because it is the exercise of our intellect not in search of truth but merely to flatter our own self-satisfaction and pride. The man who is "curious" is the one who exercises his mind not in order to glorify God but merely for the pleasure of exercising his own mind. How can such a one know the truth? He will deliberately avoid considering the facts that are displeasing to him; and the first of these facts will be his own limitations, his own failings, his own dependence upon God, his obligations toward God, and everything that reminds him of what Christian ascetical tradition, since the Gospels and St. Paul, calls his own *nothingness*—that is, his nothingness of himself, apart from God.[22]

This *curiositas* is the first degree of pride[23] and it was the cause of the fall of our first parents in Eden—the cause of the separation of the whole human race from God, and of the defilement of our own innate natural perfection of simplicity and liberty and immortality.

The serpent, in tempting Eve, told her two things: he promised her a knowledge beyond that which God had given her, and he promised her that she and Adam would be like unto gods. *"Eritis sicut dii"* (Gn 3:5).

But God had already given Adam and Eve all the knowledge that was worth having, all that really perfected their souls, all that was really true. Hence, the only addition the devil could contribute was the knowledge of evil, of falsity. In tempting them to know for the sake of their own glory and their own satisfaction, he was only offering them the useless knowledge of an untruth: he was making them a present of error, and in so doing he was acting in his true colors as the father of lies.

Non plus sapere quam oportet sapere (Rom 12:3):[24] St. Bernard applies this text to the situation in Eden—and St. Paul's words are the most eloquent of commentaries on the temptation of Eve. What is the wisdom that is fitting for us to have? The knowledge and love of truth. And what is the wisdom that we should not seek? The knowledge and love of falsity. But all knowledge that would make us "gods" is of the latter kind. And it is in that direction that we are led by *curiositas,* the love of knowledge for its own sake.

The application of this to the monastic life is too evident to need much development. Any monk who occupies himself with things that are outside his own vocation, without a justifiable and necessary cause, is on the path of *curiositas.* And one who studies even the highest and most perfect and most useful truths, theology itself, merely in order to please himself and to win honors and outshine everybody else and become famous and admired, is on the same wrong track.

But, to avoid the opposite extreme, St. Bernard would have us realize that there is another ignorance which is just as dangerous as the ignorance of our nothingness. It is paradoxically the ignorance of OUR OWN GREATNESS. This, too, we must study. It goes hand in hand with the first, and both come under the heading of that self-knowledge which grounds us in the fear of God and that knowledge of God which makes us trust in him. In the second chapter of the *De Diligendo Deo,* St. Bernard tells us explicitly that it is the ignorance of our own greatness that has reduced us to a level below the beasts of the field. If we do not know our own greatness, we will never be able to have sufficient trust in God.[25] If we do not realize that our greatness is from him, and we are nothing of ourselves, then we will not even bother to trust in God, but will rely entirely on ourselves.

That brings us back face to face with the same dilemma: presumption or despair, which we have been considering in the text from the thirty-seventh sermon on the Canticle.

3. The length of this discussion may seem only to complicate matters. To simplify them, let us consider one practical point. For St. Bernard, the first step in acquiring intellectual simplicity is the *knowledge and imitation of Christ*. Among the many places in his works where the saint develops this theme, none is more explicit than the first chapters of the *Degrees of Humility*. He begins his tract by proposing the ascent of "three degrees of truth," and each degree is appropriated to one of the Divine Persons. The first degree, humility, self-knowledge, is the one in which the work of our enlightenment is appropriated to the Incarnate Word, who sets himself before us in the Gospels as the "way, the truth, and the life" (Jn 14:6). If anyone wants a brief and practical formula that sums up St. Bernard's teaching on simplicity in the intellectual order, it is this: *"Allowing ourselves to be taught by Christ's love."*[26]

4. This intellectual simplicity, which begins with self-knowledge and the knowledge of the goodness of God as expressed by his love for us in our creation and in our redemption by Jesus Christ, paves the way for the higher simplicity of contemplation. That simplicity is even more a matter of love than of knowledge and therefore it demands a deep and searching simplification of the will that will be treated in the next selection of texts.

But we may close the present topic with a view of contemplation as it affects the intellect, operating in the extreme simplicity of an intuition that is beyond all concepts and images and pictures and phantasms and discursive acts of the mind. Here we have the visit of the Word to the soul coming in person, without the medium of thought or image or anything that we can grasp by our ordinary understanding.[27]

But here is how St. Bernard describes the visit of the Word to the soul in the simplicity of mystical contemplation.[28]

Take care lest you suppose that in this union of the Word and the soul we apprehend anything that has a body or can be imagined. . . . This union is in the spirit, because God is a spirit, and he desires the beauty of the soul of one whom he sees to be walking according to the spirit. . . . (The saint explains that such a one will never be content with ordinary or imaginary or rational apprehensions of God, or even with visions of him.) But that soul will only be content when he receives God with secret love as he descends into the soul from heaven. For then he will possess the one he desires, not in a figure, but actually infused (*non figuratum sed infusum*), not under any appearance but in the direct contact of love (*non apparentem sed afficientem*). . . . For the Divine Word is apprehended not by sound but by his actual penetration into the soul (*Verbum non sonans sed penetrans*). He makes himself heard not by speech but by direct action on the soul (*non loquax, sed efficax*), not calling out to the ears but delighting our inward love. His face is perceived not by an outward form but by the form he imposes upon our very soul (*facies non formata sed formans*).

SIMPLIFICATION OF THE WILL: OBEDIENCE

We have now seen the great danger of ignorance in the spiritual life. And yet dangerous as it may be, it can be rendered completely harmless by a *submissive and charitable will.*

If only the soul will not cling to its own lights, to its own opinion, to its own way of doing things: if only the will can bring itself to consent to hand over its judgment to a superior or competent spiritual director, and to abandon its own way for the sake of peace and the common good, *the battle for simplicity and sanctity is already won.*[1]

The discretion and counsel of the greatest saints is a mystical grace of a high order: and yet the weakest of us can possess a virtue of almost equal power and value: the virtue of simple *obedience,* which does exactly what is commanded by the superior: *nihil plus:* it adds nothing to his command by way of improvement upon it, or in order to make it a "more perfect" sacrifice. (Self-will only makes the sacrifice less perfect, and in such a case even addition is rapine in the holocaust!)[2] It adds nothing to the austerities of the Rule without permission. It fears self-chosen penances. *Nihil minus:* It is hard to say which is worse—to follow self-will in doing more than is commanded or in doing less. Both are forms of self-love. But simple obedience is always generous enough to do what is required of it, and with a good heart. *Nihil aliter*: The perfection of simplicity in obedience is to do things in the precise way that the superior wants them to be done. We can be sure of pleasing God only when we abandon all internal arguments or attempts to find an opportunity to insinuate our own will on the grounds of *in dubiis libertas*. Let us simply try our best to do exactly what our superior seems to want, what the Rule seems to require, what the other monks, especially the seniors, are doing or have done.[3]

If we were to enter into the question of obedience as it is treated by St. Bernard, we would soon pass far beyond the limits of this little book. Suffice it to make two general statements on the simplification of the will before passing to the text of St. Bernard himself.

1. Ignorance may be the ruin of simplicity and of sanctity: but only in so far as it springs from and is inseparable from pride. Obedience conquers ignorance, and even a man with the most erroneous ideas about the spiritual life can rapidly become a great saint if he places his judgment in the hands of a capable director. On the other hand, however, the greatest curse of the monastic life is the monk who not only has wrong ideas about the spiritual life, but clings to them with belligerent stubbornness and even tries to force them upon others.

2. The chief means for destroying self-will is not merely obedience. It is obedience regarded as subordinate to charity, *and as integrated in the common life.* The Cistercians were notable, among other things, for the emphasis they placed on fraternal charity and on unity in the spirit of divine love. When St. Bernard treats of the destruction of self-will, and the substitution of God's will for it, he speaks, very often, not of *voluntas Dei* but *voluntas communis*: and this common will is indeed the will of God but with an important added note: *that the will of others, the will of the community with respect to the common good of the community, the order, etc., is God's will, and to submit to our*

superiors and our brethren is to submit to God and become united to him.

This, it must be noted, is irrespective of whether our ideas may or may not be better than those of others. In all matters that do not clearly involve a fault, even when the community is wrong and the individual is right, he can best keep united with God by following the *voluntas communis*[4] for the sake of peace and charity.

The chief characteristic of *voluntas propria* is, as we have seen (Text 1), a spirit of separation, of self-exaltation in a private heaven which belongs to us alone, by our own right, where we are our own gods, and where neither God nor man can interfere with our self-complacent desires. The type of this pride is the Pharisee of the parable (Lk 18:11). To avoid falling into his sin, we must use the knowledge we have acquired of ourselves (Text 2) to learn that we are no better than others, and that we suffer as they do, and they suffer as we do, and that we all need the grace of God. This substitution of compassion for suspicion, intolerance, or contempt is a necessary degree in the ascent of the soul to mystical union with God which, to St. Bernard, is unthinkable unless the soul is first prepared and purified by a true and deep and universal and supernatural love for other men.

These truths are all reflected or included in the great third sermon for paschal time, one of St. Bernard's most important expositions of his doctrine on the active purification of the will.

The subject is the purification of the leper Naaman (2 Kgs 5:10).

From Sermon 3 for Easter:

> There is, in the heart, a twofold leprosy: our own will and our own judgment. Our own will (*voluntatem propriam*), I call that which is not common to us and God and other men but is ours alone.[5] That is, when we carry out our will, not for the honor of God, nor for the benefit of our neighbor, but simply for ourselves alone. Self-will means to will things that are intended not to give pleasure to God

or to be of use to our brethren, but only to satisfy the selfish promptings of our own minds. Diametrically opposed to this evil is charity: and charity is God.

Self-will, then, is ever in a state of implacable hostility to God and constantly wages the *most cruel warfare against him*. What is there that God hates or punishes except self-will?

If self-will were to cease to exist, there would be no more hell. For what fuel would there be to feed those flames if there were no self-will?[6] Even now in this life, when we feel the cold or hunger or other such things, what is it that feels the suffering if not self-will? For if we willingly bear with these trials, our will becomes the *common will*. What may be called our own will is really a kind of sickness and corruption of the true will: and it is this corrupt element that will continue to be the subject of every kind of suffering until it is totally consumed.[7]

But now let those who are slaves to self-will hear and fear with how great fury self-will attacks the Lord of majesty. To begin with, it subtracts and withdraws itself from his domination and becomes its own master when, by right, it should serve the God who made it. But will it be content to stop at this offense? By no means: its next step is to do all in its power to tear away from God and to destroy everything that is his. What limit does human greed avow? Is it not true that the man who by usury has acquired a moderate sum of money would go on to gain the whole world if it were possible, and if his will could only find the way to do it? . . . Not only that, but self-will does all that it can to destroy God himself. For there is nothing it would like better than to have God either unable or unwilling to punish its sins, or else to have him ignorant of them. But when self-will would have God to be powerless, or unjust, or ignorant, that is the same as willing him not to be God. And that is the closest the will can come to destroying God. . . . This, then, is that most filthy leprosy of the soul on account of which we have to bathe in the Jordan and imitate him who came not to do his own will, whence in his very passion he cried out: Not my will but thine be done!

Remarks

We interrupt this crucial text at the end of its first convenient division to make a few comments necessary to tie it in more closely with the theme of this book.

1. Self-will is in the *intention* to please ourselves: (*non intendentes placere Deo . . . sed satisfacere propriis motibus animorum*). First, it must be made clear that self-will and the common will are not two separate faculties of the soul. There is only one will, but it can act in two diametrically opposed ways. Self-will and the common will are two mutually contradictory modes of action. And what must be stressed above all is the fact that it is the *common will that is natural to us* and self-will is simply a perversion.

By *intention*, St. Bernard is speaking of the actual movement of the will toward what is, in real fact, its chosen object. He is not speaking of the intention which may exist in our imagination or on our lips, and which may be a self-delusion produced in a conscience completely warped and blinded by our own pride, as when the Jews crucified Christ "that the people might not perish."

What is meant by an *intention to please ourselves*? St. Bernard says it is an act of the will moving primarily toward the satisfaction of our own desires. The will acts simply because we want this, we like that, we think this is right, we feel like doing such and such a thing. It is not always easy to say when such motives are the ones behind our acts until these desires come in conflict with (a) God's signified will, laws, rules, orders of superiors, duties, and obligations; (b) the will or desires or interests of others; (c) providential circumstances, etc. *If such obstacles destroy our peace of mind, cause us to rebel, to get excited, to lose our tempers, or to become depressed, despondent, or, finally, to override the will of God and man alike to get our own way,* then we have clear evidence that our intention was more or less selfish (in proportion to the disturbance) no matter what fine reasons we may have given for our act beforehand.[8]

2. *Charitas . . . quae Deus est.* This is an extremely strong sentence. But it is true. The common will is a participation in the life of God for it is charity. It is God's will, God's *love*, the *vinculum pacis,* the bond of peace uniting men to one another and to God himself. By this shall all men know we are Christ's disciples, if we love one another. And again, if we love him, we will keep his commandments. The case is perfectly clear from our Lord's address to his disciples at the Last Supper (Jn 14–17). Consequently, if we want union with God, let us obey our superiors and give in to one another, honoring one another, and seeking to do what is profitable to others, not what happens to suit our own pleasure or convenience.[9] This is true simplicity, because it destroys diversity of wills and unites a multiplicity of characters and dispositions and interests in the harmony of one love, the bond of peace.

3. There is a well-regulated self-love, namely that which seeks the perfection of our own nature in the manner destined for it by God.[10] This alone should be enough to turn us away from the intolerable burden of unhappiness imposed by the unnatural tyranny of self-will. Self-will is the cause of all unhappiness, the subject of all unhappiness. This is a favorite theme with the Cistercian fathers.[11] Why? Because, for our fathers, unhappiness resided essentially in the conflict of our will with the will of God, with our brothers, with Providence, etc. Hence, *lack of peace is identified with a certain lack of simplicity, a lack of union, of harmony with circumstances and events.* Simplicity thus takes on the sense of *abandonment.* But even so-called passive abandonment in our fathers was always so markedly *positive* in its act that it was never a merely passive acceptance of God's will, but *an active desire that God's will be done.*[12] This in itself is a more perfect union with God, a more perfect simplicity. There was no quietistic apathy at Clairvaux.

4. Finally, it is necessary to stress the fact that self-will is a corruption of our natural freedom, our natural simplicity. In the

last analysis, true simplicity for us can only mean the struggle to eliminate self-will and its concomitant, our own judgment (*proprium consilium*), the subject of the next division of the third sermon in paschal time.

SIMPLIFICATION OF THE WILL: OUR OWN JUDGMENT

Now the leprosy of our own judgment is all the more dangerous, for it is the more hidden: and the more we have of it, the more we appear, to ourselves, to be healthy. This is the disease of those who have the zeal of God, but not according to knowledge for they cling obstinately to their own errors to such an extent that they cannot bear to take advice from anybody else.

These are the kind who break up the unity of the Church or of the monastery, and are the enemies of peace, men without charity, puffed up with vanity, and thoroughly pleased with themselves, great in their own eyes, ignoring the justice of God, and desiring *to set up their own standard of justice in its place.*

And what greater pride is there than that one man should try to impose his own opinion upon the whole community, as if he alone had the spirit of God? Refusal to obey is the crime of idolatry and to resist is like unto witchcraft.[1] Woe, then, to those who make themselves out to be holier than everybody else, who are not like unto other men. . . .

An excerpt from a beautiful passage on the same topic, Sermon 46 on the Canticle of Canticles, paragraph six, comes in appropriately at this point:[2]

> Indeed I am amazed at the impudence of some monks among us, who, after they have upset the entire community with their singularities, have irritated us with their impatience, condemned us with their rebelliousness and their bad tempers, nevertheless dare to aspire, with the most fervent prayers, to mystical union with the Lord of all purity. . . . The centurion begged the Lord not to enter under his roof, because of his own unworthiness: and yet the fame of his faith went out through all Israel: and these men would compel him to enter into their dwelling, vile with the filth of such great vices?
>
> What would you have me do, such a one will ask. I would have you first of all cleanse your conscience of every stain of anger and quarrelsomeness, of murmuring and of bad temper and hasten to drive out of your heart whatever goes against peace with your brethren or obedience to your superiors. Then to adorn and prepare yourself with good works, with praiseworthy thoughts, with the sweet odor of virtues. . . .[3]

Returning to the third sermon in paschal time, we find the saint even more explicit in his prescription of a remedy for *proprium consilium*. He silences all objections, at least on the part of those who call themselves Christians, by the example of the obedience of Christ, who submitted his own infinite wisdom to the judgments and wills of two of his creatures, Our Lady and St. Joseph:

> But where can this leprosy be cleansed except in the Jordan (that is, in the humility of Christ)? Whosoever thou art that art thus afflicted, bathe therein, and observe what was done by the angel of great counsel and how he subjected his counsel to the counsel, or rather to the will of one woman: the Blessed Virgin, and to the will of a poor carpenter, Joseph (cf. Lk 2:46–51).[4]
>
> Who then would not be ashamed to cling obstinately to his own judgment when wisdom himself gave up *his* judgment?

But perhaps we ought to inquire of him how it is that he gave up his will and abandoned his counsel.

The saint here passes to the agony in the Garden and the problem of the divergence between the will of Christ as man, and his Father's will. Was there, then, self-will in our Lord? Not in the sense of the corrupt mode of willing of which the saint has spoken above. That would be impossible. However, he did have his own human will.

> Lord, concerning thy will, which thou didst say should not be done: if it was not good, how could it have been thy will? But if it was good, then why did it have to be given up? In the same way, concerning thy judgment: if it was not right, how could it have been thy judgment—and if it was right, why should it be given up? Both the will and the judgment were good, and they were both his: but it was nonetheless right that they be given up, in order that something better still might be accomplished. Therefore, when Christ said: "If it be possible, let this chalice pass from me" (Mt 26:39), that was his will, and it was good. But the will with which he said *"Thy will be done"* was better because it was common to the Father, to Christ himself (since he was offered up because he himself willed it), and to us. For unless the grain of wheat, falling into the ground had died, itself would have remained alone: but dying, it bore much fruit.
>
> And this was the *will of the Father*: that he should have many whom he could adopt as *his* sons. It was *Christ's will* to be the firstborn of many brethren, and it was *our will*, because it was on our behalf that he did this thing, that we might be redeemed. The same may be said regarding his judgment. When Christ said: "I must be about my Father's business," that was his judgment, and it was good. But because Mary and Joseph did not understand, he changed his mind, in order to cleanse us of the leprosy of attachment to our own judgment.

Remarks

1. In the first place, the distinction between corrupt self-will and well-regulated self-will now becomes apparent. The

natural desire to avoid pain, to preserve life, etc., is in itself simply a movement of the sense appetite, and therefore in itself indifferent. We must not confuse the sense appetite with the will, still less must we regard it as a sort of an "evil will." This was the mistake of the Albigensian heretics, against whom St. Bernard preached so vehemently. When Christ as man felt a desire to avoid the sufferings of Calvary which were not even strictly necessary to redeem us and which he was under no obligation to undergo, to have given the consent of his will to such repugnance would not have been an evil, but a good act in the natural order. It would have been perfectly reasonable, perfectly prudent, to avoid an unjust and cruel death, if God had not willed otherwise.

2. This brings us to the most important topic, of that "social simplicity" which we call charity or the *common will*.

No matter from what angle we approach Cistercian simplicity, the core and essence of it always turns out to be one thing: LOVE. The will, for St. Bernard as for all the Augustinians, is man's highest faculty. Therefore the highest and most perfect simplicity attainable by intelligent beings is a union of wills. The all-embracing union of charity, which is effected by the Holy Ghost himself, unites men to God and men to men in God in the most perfect and simple union of one loving will, which is God's own will, the *voluntas communis*. This union is what Christ died to purchase for us. It is the work of his Spirit in us, and to realize it perfectly is to be in heaven: indeed the whole work of achieving this final magnificent and universal simplicity of all men made one in Christ will be his eventual triumph at the last day.

3. Hence we see that the very essence of Cistercian simplicity is the practice of charity and loving obedience and mutual patience and forbearance in the community life which should be, on earth, an image of the simplicity of heaven. *We now begin to see something of the depth of this beautiful Cistercian ideal!*

On the other hand, the devil is always working to break up this simplicity, to break the order down into separate groups, the groups into conflicting houses, the houses into cliques, and the cliques into warring individuals. St. Stephen's Charter of Charity was explicitly directed against this work of hell.[5]

The chief weapon used by the devil in this conflict is our own corrupt self-will, our self-judgment, and the two together are commonly called pride, which makes us idolaters, self-worshippers, and consequently *unitatis divisores*, disrupters of union, destroyers of simplicity.

Cistercian simplicity, then, begins in humility and self-distrust, and climbs through obedience to the perfection of fraternal charity to produce that unity and peace by which the holy and undivided Trinity is reflected not only in the individual soul but in the community, in the order, in the Church of God. Once a certain degree of perfection in this social simplicity is arrived at on earth, God is pleased to bend down and raise up the individuals who most further this unity by their humility and love to a closer and far more intimate union with him by mystical prayer, mystical union.

The culmination of Cistercian simplicity is the mystical marriage of the soul with God, which is nothing else but the perfect union of our will with God's will, made possible by the complete purification of all the duplicity of error and sin. This purification is the work of love and particularly of the love of God in our neighbor. Hence it is inseparable from that social simplicity which consists in living out the *voluntas communis* in actual practice. This is the reason for the Cistercian insistence on the common life: the Cistercian is almost never physically alone. He has opportunities to give up his will to others twenty-four hours a day. It is precisely this which, according to the mind of St. Bernard, St. Aelred, and our other fathers, *should prepare him most rapidly for the mystical marriage.*[6]

All this may be made plain in one final quotation, before passing on to the consideration of that ultimate perfection of simplicity which is the mystical marriage.

In his first sermon on the feast of St. Michael and All Angels, St. Bernard depicts the solicitude of the heavenly spirits for the perfection of this work of simplification which makes the Church on earth like that in heaven, a perfect union of souls in loving and praising God.

From Sermon 1.5 on the feast of St. Michael and All Angels:

> There are many things which please the angels, and which it delights them to see in us, like sobriety, chastity, voluntary poverty, repeated sighs of desire for heaven, prayers accompanied with tears and with the heart truly directed to God. But above all these things, the angels of peace look to find among us unity and peace. Is it surprising that they should take the greatest delight of all in these two things which show forth, as it were, the form of their own heavenly city among us, and allow them to behold their new Jerusalem here on earth? And so I say, that just as that heavenly city "participates in the selfsame,"[7] so let us also think the same, say the same things, and let there not be divisions among us: but rather let us all together form one body in Christ, being all members one of another.[8]
>
> On the other hand, there is nothing so offensive to these heavenly spirits, and nothing which so moves them to indignation as dissensions and scandals, when such things are found among us. For let us hear the words of Paul to the Corinthians: "When there is jealousy and contention among you, are you not carnal, and do you not walk according to man?" (1 Cor 3:3). And in the Epistle of Jude the Apostle we read: "These are they who segregate themselves, brute beasts, not having the Spirit of God" (Jude 19). Consider the soul of man, how it gives life to all the members of the body in their union one with another. But separate any one member from its union with the rest, and see how long it will continue to receive life from the soul! . . . That is what happens to every man who is cut off from unity with other men: *there can be no doubt that the Spirit of Life withdraws from such a one.* It is very just, then, that the apostles should call contentious men, and those who separate themselves[9] from others, carnal men and brute beasts, who have not the Spirit of God. And the saints and the blessed spirits in heaven say, when they come upon scandals and dissensions: "What have we to do with this generation that hath not the Spirit?" For if the Spirit were

there, charity would be everywhere diffused by him, and
unity would not be broken.

The last sentence makes it once more perfectly clear that the
operation of the *voluntas communis* and the operation of the
Holy Ghost are one and the same thing, and the man who
wishes to become united to the Holy Ghost only has to enter
into participation in this unity of charity by humbly giving up
whatever is disordered in his own will to that of the Church,
the order, his superiors, his individual brethren, and through
all these to God. Sanctified by this participation in the common
will which is God himself working in men and in the Church,
the individual monk is prepared for the graces of infused
contemplation.

PERFECT SIMPLICITY: UNITY OF SPIRIT WITH GOD

We remember how, as we began this ascent of the holy soul to God, St. Bernard told us that the fundamental thing was the recognition of God's image in ourselves: the end was to be the perfect rehabilitation of that image, in all its simplicity, in the purity of its original likeness to God. Now that this likeness is finally to be recovered by perfect love and confidence,[1] it is fitting that we consider just how much it means.

This likeness produces more than a similarity between two separate objects. It takes the soul and makes it one with God: so close is this unity of the soul with God, that it is said *to become God*. The Divine Essence can never belong to us by nature and we shall always remain distinct, substantially, from God. But in the union of love which God has prepared for those that love him and seek him, everything that is his will become ours, not by nature *but by grace*.

We cannot, then, become one substance with God. But the union that we can achieve with him is only one degree less perfect than this. The union *of wills*, making us one spirit with God, is the highest and purest and most intimate union that can possibly be achieved by two individuals remaining essentially distinct.

This is the culminating ideal of Cistercian simplicity!

The paradox is that the soul itself is more perfectly simple when absorbed in this union than it could ever be outside of it. The soul is never so truly itself as it is when it is lost in God and it is never so unlike itself as when it is completely separated from God and left entirely to itself. The reason for this paradox is in the fact that it is of the very essence of the soul to be like God and therefore it is most truly itself when it becomes, as nearly as is possible to a creature, *identified with him.*

In this perfect identification of the soul with God the soul is rightly said to lose itself in God: not in the sense of losing its substance, but in the sense of losing its *own will* in a perfect union of love with God's will that makes them truly one will, one spirit.

In such a state, the soul has *completely forgotten itself and its own interests and desires* for the simple reason that it no longer has any interests or desires other than those of God. It no longer has anything whatever of its own. It retains its own substance, but now it loves that substance with God's love rather than its own. The soul in this supereminent perfection of simplicity *now loves itself exactly as God loves it,* in the same degree, in the same manner—indeed, with the very same love. Even self-love is at last vindicated in this ultimate beatification of the soul! That is of course because the illusory personality, the false self-superimposed upon the divine image by sin, has now been utterly destroyed in the successive purifications by the humiliating truth and by union with the *voluntas communis* (common will) in obedience and charity.

St. Bernard describes this union in the tenth chapter of the *De Diligendo Deo*:

> But when shall flesh and blood, this vessel of clay, this earthly dwelling, attain at last to this fourth degree of

love?[2] When shall the soul experience this desire (*affectum*) to the extent of becoming inebriated with divine love and, forgetting itself, becoming to itself like a lost vessel[3] so that it may pass over entirely into God and, adhering to God, become one spirit with him and say: My flesh and my heart hath fainted away, thou are the God of my heart, and the God that is my portion forever.[4]

I should call that man holy and blessed, to whom it may be granted to experience such love, even were it only rarely, or but once, and that in a brief flash (*raptim*) which might pass and be all over in an instant. For to lose yourself, in a manner of speaking, and to become as though you did not exist, and to lose absolutely all consciousness of yourself, and to go forth from yourself, and to be practically annihilated, all that belongs to heaven and is utterly above natural human love (*coelestis est conversationis, non humanae affectionis*).

The saint laments the fact that one must come back to earth, to the necessities of one's own body, and to the duties of the active life, after such an experience, then continues:

However, since Holy Scripture says that God made all things for himself (Prv 16:4), the creature must surely at some time conform itself to its Creator.[5] Someday, then, we must attain to the same love that God has for us. We must reach the point where, just as God willed all things to exist only for himself, so we too may will to have existed and to exist, and will everything else to have been or to be solely for the sake of God and on account of his will alone, not for our own pleasure. We shall then delight, not in the fact that all our needs have been satisfied, and all our happiness carried to the ultimate consummation *but in the fact that his will in us and for us will then be seen to be completely accomplished and carried out.*[6] And this is what we daily ask for in our prayers when we say: Thy will be done on earth as it is in heaven. O holy and chaste love! O sweet and delightful affection! *O pure, utterly clean intention of the will, all the cleaner and more pure because no admixture of self remains* therein; all the sweeter and more delightful in that what we feel is entirely divine. To love like this is to become a god. *Sic affici deificari est.*

This, then, is the ultimate limit of Cistercian simplicity: the simplicity of God himself, belonging to the soul, purified of all admixture of self-love, admitted to a participation in the Divine Nature, and becoming one spirit with the God of infinite love.

AFTERWORD BY
ABBOT ELIAS DIETZ,
O.C.S.O.

The 1948 edition of *The Spirit of Simplicity* ended with a conclusion in which Thomas Merton encourages readers to undertake further reading and study, especially on the early documents of the order. Since most of the information he provided is now out of date, that short text is not included here. Nonetheless, his main point remains valid and is worth citing: "We can never hope to acquire the spirit of simplicity characteristic of our order if we never enter into contact, directly or at least indirectly, with the sources from which it flowed." So it seems opportune to include here an update on the many resources that have become available in the intervening years.

Regarding the early documents of the order, especially the *Exordium Parvum* and the Charter of Charity, good English translations of these texts are available on the order's website (www.ocso.org). Along with these texts, an entire program of initiation into these early documents titled *Exordium*, prepared by Fr. Michael Casey, is available on the same site.

The standard critical text of the early documents is now Fr. Chrysogonus Waddell's *Narrative and Legislative Texts from Early Cîteaux* (Cîteaux-Commentarii cistercienses, 1999), which contains extensive introductions and commentaries along with English translations of all the texts. Fr. Waddell also edited the *Twelfth-century Statues from the Cistercian General Chapter: Latin Text with English Notes and Commentary* (Cîteaux-Commentarii cistercienses, 2002), and a volume entitled *Cistercian Lay Brothers: Twelfth-Century Usages with Related Texts: Latin Text with Concordance of Latin Terms, English Translations and Notes* (Cîteaux-Commentarii cistercienses, 2000). As for the earliest Cistercian customary or usages, the standard resource is Danièle Choisselet and Placide Vernet, eds., *Les Ecclesiastica officia cisterciens du XIIe siècle: Texte latin selon les manuscrits édités de Trente 1711, Ljubljana 31 et Dijon 114, version française, annexe liturgique, notes index et tables,* Choisselet D., Vernet P. ed. (Abbaye d'Oelenberg: La Documentation cistercienne, 1989).

In his concluding remarks in the 1948 edition of *The Spirit of Simplicity* Thomas Merton also encourages readers to go further afield and discover the order's major authors such as Bernard of Clairvaux, William of Saint Thierry, and Aelred of Rievaulx, lamenting the fact that there were so few books in English at the time. Thanks to initiatives within the order such as *The Spirit of Simplicity* and the inspiration of figures such as Chautard and Merton, scholars and translators have since made a great deal of progress in the recovery of the Cistercian heritage and in making it accessible in all the major languages.

A large proportion of the writings of the early Cistercians is now available in English in the Cistercian Fathers Series (currently published by Cistercian Publications in collaboration with Liturgical Press), which has reached more than seventy volumes. In addition, a related collection titled Cistercian Studies Series consists of more than 250 volumes. The journal *Cistercian Studies Quarterly* is now in its fifty-second year.

ABBREVIATIONS

Apo   *An Apologia to Abbot William* (*Apologia ad Guillelmum abbatem*) by St. Bernard
CC   *Carta caritatis* (the *Charter of Charity*)
CF   Cistercian Fathers Series (Cistercian Publications)
CS   Cistercian Studies Series (Cistercian Publications)
Dil   *On Loving God* (*De diligendo Deo*) by St. Bernard
Div   *Monastic Sermons* (*Sermones de diversis*) by St. Bernard
EP   *Exordium parvum* (often called the *Little Exordium* in the text)
Ep frat *The Golden Epistle* (*Epistola ad Fratres de Monte Dei*) by William of Saint Thierry
Miss   Homilies in Praise of the Blessed Virgin Mary (*Homilia super "Missus est" in laudibus virginis matris*) by St. Bernard
MW   Monastic Wisdom Series (Cistercian Publications)
NLTEC Chrysogonus Waddell, ed., *Narrative and Legislative Texts from Early Cîteaux* (Cîteaux-Commentarii cistercienses, 1999)
RB   Rule of St. Benedict
SC   *Sermons on the Song of Songs* (*Sermones in Cantica*) by St. Bernard

NOTES

Preface

1. See Merton's brief biographical note on Dom Frederic Dunne from October 1946: *Entering the Silence: Becoming a Monk and Writer*, ed. Jonathan Montaldo, The Journals of Thomas Merton, vol. 2, 1941–1952 (San Francisco: HarperCollins, 1996). I am grateful to Dr. Paul Pearson, director of the Merton Center at Bellarmine University, Louisville, for help in locating various references to *The Spirit of Simplicity* in Merton's writings.

2. In *The Sign of Jonas* (May 1, 1947), he says about this job: "I am not quite sure what has happened to the six- and seven-hundred-page lives of Cistercian saints which I wrote as a novice, freezing to death in the unheated library." Fortunately, this work is now available under the title *In the Valley of Wormwood: Cistercian Blessed and Saints of the Golden Age*, Cistercian Studies Series 233 (Collegeville: Liturgical Press, 2013).

3. On October 9, 1950, he wrote to Dom Jean Leclercq: "A copy of *The Spirit of Simplicity* was mailed to you, but my own contribution to that work is confused and weak, I believe. I refer to the second part." See *Survival of Prophecy? The Correspondence of Jean Leclercq and Thomas Merton*, ed. Patrick Hart, Monastic Wisdom Series 17 (Collegeville: Cistercian Publications, 2008), 17.

4. Jean Leclercq considered Merton's part 2 of *The Spirit of Simplicity* to be "a good summary of St. Bernard's theology." See his introductory remarks in *Thomas Merton on St. Bernard*, Cistercian Studies Series 9 (Kalamazoo: Cistercian Publications, 1980), 16–18.

5. Hugues Séjalon, ed., Nomasticon Cisterciense seu Antiquiores Ordinis Cisterciensis Constitutiones . . . , Solesmes, 1892.

6. Philippe Guignard, ed., *Les monuments primitifs de la règle cistercienne publiés d'après les manuscrits de l'Abbaye de Cîteaux, Dijon,* 1878.

Foreword

1. Note that although the contemplative may be dispensed from actual preaching, he is never, and never can be, dispensed from the *apostolate*. He is bound in duty to do everything he can to spread the Gospel of Christ: not by the spoken or written word, but by more effective means: prayer and sacrifice.

2. This is very well explained in the first section of the following report.

3. Ep frat 1.13.49 [CF 12:28]. William of Saint Thierry was born in Liege, Belgium, about 1085. Having made profession as a Benedictine monk in France, he became abbot of the monastery of St. Thierry, near Rheims. He soon came under the influence of St. Bernard of Clairvaux and the Cistercian reform, and he was able, in his turn, to inspire the abbot of Clairvaux by his conversations and ideas. St. Bernard dedicated his *Apologia* for Cistercian simplicity against the Cluniacs to William of Saint Thierry, who shared his views to such an extent that he himself became a Cistercian at the monastery of Signy where he continued to write on the spiritual life. It was there that he died on the eighth of September, the Nativity of Our Lady, eight hundred years ago, in 1148.

Part 1
Introduction

1. *Novi milites Christi cum paupere Christo pauperes . . . ut . . . tenacius . . . observantiam Sanctae Regulae ament . . . in arcta et angusta via quam Regula demonstrat . . . desudent . . . —Vitam suam sub custodia Sanctae Regulae Patris Benedicti se ordinaturos pollicentes. . . .* ["The new soldiers of Christ, poor with the poor Christ . . . in order . . . more tenaciously . . . might love the observance of the Holy Rule . . . in the straight and narrow way which the Rule points out . . . may sweat and toil . . . —Their intention to order their life under the custody of the Holy Rule of our Father Benedict . . ."] [a collage of expressions from various places in the EP].

Regulae Beatissimi Benedicti quam . . . tepide ac negligenter . . . tenueratis, arctius deinceps atque perfectius inhaerere . . . ["You wished from then on to adhere more strictly and perfectly to the Rule of the most blessed Benedict, which till then you had observed lukewarmly and negligently."] (Letter of the Legate Hugh, at Lyons, to St. Robert and his companions, as they were about to leave Molesme) [EP 2.3; NLTEC 419].

2. This date, 1119, is the one generally accepted (cf. Dom Anselme Le Bail, *L'Ordre de Cîteaux—La Trappe*, p. 32) but there are serious reasons for thinking that the Charter of Charity was approved by the Chapter of 1117 or 1118.

1. Interior Simplicity

1. "If he truly seeks God," RB 58. (This is the first thing the novice master, according to St. Benedict, must find out about the

postulant who presents himself at the monastery, seeking admission.
—*Translator*)

2. *Simplex natura simplicitatem cordis exquirit.* ["Simplicity of nature seeks simplicity of heart."] Div 37.9 [=Sermon 3 on the Time of Harvest; CF 54:13].

3. Two fine texts from St. Augustine's *De Vera Religione* have inspired our thoughts. The first shows us the soul *divided*, and, as it were, broken in pieces as a consequence of the Fall: *Temporalium enim specierum multiformitas ab unitate Dei hominem lapsum per carnales sensus diverberavit, et mutabili varietate multiplicavit ejus affectum. . . . Sic multiplicatus est ut non inveniat Naturam Incommutabilem et Singularem, quam secutus non erret et assecutus non doleat* (21.41). Translation: "The multiplicity of temporal things, shattered man, who had fallen because of his carnal senses, and multiplied his desires by variety and change. . . . He was multiplied in such a way that he became unable to find the One and Changeless Nature, to follow whom would have meant the end of wandering, and to find whom is the end of suffering."

The second text shows us the soul returning from creatures to God through simplicity: *Si autem, dum in hoc stadio vitae humanae anima degit, vincat eas, quas adversum se nutrivit, cupiditates, et ad eas vincendas gratia Dei se adjuvari credat, mente Illi serviens et bona voluntate, sine dubitatione reparabitur, et a multis mutabilibus ad Unum Incommutabile revertetur . . . frueturque Deo per Spiritum Sanctum, quod est Donum Dei* (12.24). Translation: "But if, while the soul still remains in the arena of human life, it overcomes the desires which it has bred up to be its own enemies, and believes that it is aided in overcoming them, by the grace of God, serving him with ready mind and good will, it will, beyond all doubt, be put together again, and will get back from the multiplicity of changing things to the changeless One . . . and will enjoy God through the Holy Ghost, who is the Gift of God."

4. *Ut sint consummati in unum.* "That they may be made perfect in one" (Jn 17:23).

5. Pseudo-Dionysius, *De Divinis Nominibus*, 4.9.

6. *Qui autem adhaeret Domino unus spiritus est* (1 Cor 6:17).

7. *Cui omnia unum sunt, et qui omnia ad unum trahit, et omnia in uno videt, potest stabilis corde esse et in Deo pacificus permanere. Imitation of Christ*, 1.3.2.

8. Μοναχός: alone, single, simple.

9. *De Eccles.*, Hierch., 6.1.3.

10. Ibid., 2.3.5.

11. Ibid., 6.2.

12. Ibid., 6.3.1.

13. Ibid., 2.3.5.

14. *Apertis oculis nostris ad deificum lumen* (RB, Prol.).

15. *Quisquis ergo ad patriam caelestem festinas . . .* (RB 73).

16. *Ut recto cursu perveniamus ad Creatorem nostrum* (Ibid.).

17. St. Thomas says: "Purity is necessary if the soul is to be united with God, because as soon as it is attached to inferior things, it becomes sullied, in the same way that every being is sullied by becoming mingled with something of lesser worth than itself: for instance, silver is impure when mixed with lead. Since it is necessary that the soul become detached from inferior things in order to be able to be united to what is above it, it follows that, without purity, it cannot become attached to God" (2a, 2ae, Q. 81, Art. 8).

18. *De Divinis Nominibus*, 13.3.

19. St. Gregory the Great (*Moralia*, 1.39), says: *Thymiama ex aromatibus compositum facimus, cum in altari boni operis virtutum multiplicitate redolemus.* "We make a compound of all aromatic herbs when, at the altar of good works, we burn the incense of all the different virtues." (Cf. Ex 30:34, where we read of the compound that was burned on the altar of incense.)

20. Pseudo-Dionysius, *De Eccles.* Hierch., 2.3.8.

21. *Ut ad eum per obedientiae laborem redeas . . .* (RB, Prol.).

22. *Omnes magistram sequantur regulam* (RB 3).

23. *Super omnia charitatem habete, quod est vinculum perfectionis.* "Above all, have charity, which is the bond of perfection" (Col 3:14). *Quia scilicet omnes virtutes quodammodo ligat in unitatem perfectam.* St. Thomas, 2a, 2ae, Q. 184, Art. 1: "For it binds together all the other virtues into a perfect unity."

24. *Nihil sibi Christo carius existimant* (RB 5).

25. *Abnegare semetipsum sibi, ut sequatur* Christum (RB 4).

26. *Sit igitur etiam in nobis, charissimi, unitas animorum; unita sint corda diligendo Unum, quaerendo Unum, adhaerendo Uni, et idipsum invicem sentientes* (Sermon 2 in Septuag.). Cf. [below, in part 2] "St. Bernard of Clairvaux on Interior Simplicity," Text 3.—*Translator*

2. Being True to Our Ideals

1. *A fonte praecide rivum, praecisus arescit* (De Unit. Ecclesiae). "Consider the rock whence you were hewn," says Isaiah, "and the quarry whence you have been drawn" (Is 51:1).

2. Collect for the feast of St. Bernard, and for his votive office.

3. Conc. Vat., Schema I, Constit. de Regul.

4. *Ut si quando a sancto proposito et observantia sanctae Regulae declinare, quod absit, tentaverint, per nostram sollicitudinem ad rectitudinem vitae redire possint* (Carta Char., Nomasticon, p. 69) [CC 1.5; NLTEC 443].

5. *DEI OPERI quod coepistis manum nostrae confirmationis apponimus* (Confirm, Carta Char., Nomasticon, p. 74) [NLTEC 451].

6. *Nunc vero volumus, illisque praecipimus, ut regulam Beati Benedicti per omnia observent, sicuti in Novo Monasterio observatur. Non alium inducant sensum in lectionem sanctae Regulae; sed sicut antecessores nostri sancti patres, monachi scilicet Novi Monasterii, intellexerunt et tenuerunt, et nos hodie intelligimus et tenemus: ita et isti intelligant et teneant* (Carta Char., 2. Nomasticon, p. 69) [CC 2; NLTEC 444].

3. Simplicity in the Little Exoridum

1. The original *Usages*, compiled under the direction of St. Stephen Harding, with a few additions after his death.

2. *In terris, in vineis ac pratis curtibusque eadem Ecclesia crevit* (Exord. Parv., 17. Nom., p. 64) [EP 17.9; NLTEC 438].

3. The *Exordium Magnum* is a much longer book than the former, and of much less historical authority; but it is nevertheless a work of major importance to anyone seeking to understand the spirit of the early Cistercians. It was evidently not all written at the same time or by the same author. (On this point see Vacandard, *Vie de Saint Bernard*, Introd., p. xlviii.) The most interesting sections are books 2–6, written at Clairvaux shortly after the time of St. Bernard, and filled with details of the saint's life, together with authentic accounts of the edifying lives of various monks and brothers of the golden age at Clairvaux. The later sections are of more obscure origin, and their value is less certain. The *Exordium Magnum* is found in Migne, *Patrologia Latina*, vol. 185, and is available in a French translation, published by La Grande Trappe. Most of the stories have found their way into the Cistercian menology, like that of the brother who pleased God more by his simple prayers while watching the sheep at a distant grange, where he was kept by obedience during the night of the feast of the Assumption, than all the monks and brethren in choir at the distant abbey, whose devotion he offered to God in tears in his humility *and* isolation from them. —*Translator*

4. *Instituta monachorum Cisterciensium de Molismo verieentium — Abbas, ille et fratres ejus Regulam beati Benedicti in illo loco ordinare et unanimiter statuerunt tenere* (Exord. Parv., Nomast., p. 62) [EP 15.1–2; NLTEC 434].

5. Dijon, 1878. He prints all the basic documents, the manuscript of the Rule, the *Little Exordium*, the *Carta Caritatis, Consuetudines, Kalendarium* (Martyrology), etc., from the monastery of Cîteaux, and now in the public library of Dijon. He also adds the usages of the nuns of Tart and other interesting material in medieval French.

6. Pages xvii–xxv of this preface force us to conclude that the primitive regulations were, first of all, the *Instituta* set down in the *Exordium*, and that they were submitted to Pope Callixtus II, and approved by him at the same time as the Charter of Charity.

7. *Ecce hujus saeculi divitiis spretis, coeperunt novi milites Christi, cum paupere Christo pauperes, inter se tractare quo ingenio quove artificio seu quo exercitio in hac vita se hospitesque divites et pauperes supervenientes, quos ut Christum suscipere praecipit regula, sustentarent* (loc. cit., p. 63) [EP 15.9; NLTEC 435].

8. *Qui nec in regula nec in vita Sancti Benedicti* eumdem doctorem legebant possedisse ecclesias, vel altaria, seu oblationes, aut sepulturas, vel decimas aliorum hominum, seu furnos, vel molendina, atit villas vel rusticos; nec etiam feminas monasterium ejus intrasse, nec, mortuos ibidem, excepta sorore sua sepelisse, ideo haec omnia abdicaverunt* (loc. cit., p. 62.) [EP 15.5; NLTEC 434].

*The *Life of St. Benedict* here referred to is the one fundamental source of all information about the Patriarch of the Monks of the West, written by St. Gregory the Great, and included in his *Dialogues*. This life itself is one of the masterpieces of biography of all time and is above all remarkable for its simplicity, which gives it a character of inimitable dignity and charm. There is no better way of cultivating this virtue than by meditating on this beautiful work. —*Translator*

9. *Non immemores sponsionis suae, Regulam Beati Benedicti in loco illo ordinare et unanimiter statuerunt tenere* (Ibid.) [EP 15.2; NLTEC 434].

10. *Ubi beatus pater Benedictus docet ut monachus a saecularibus actibus se faciat alienum, ibi liquido testatur haec non debere versari in actibus vel cordibus monachorum, qui nominis sui etymologiam haec fugiendo sectari debent* (Ibid.) [EP 15.5–6; NLTEC 434–435].

11. *Contristabantur, videntes se caeterosque monachos hanc regulam solemni professione servaturos, promisse, eamque minime custodisse.* "They became sorrowful when they beheld how they, and the other monks, having promised to keep the Rule at their profession had, in fact, not been doing so at all" (*Little Exordium*, c. 3, Nom., p. 55) [EP 3.6; NLTEC 421].

12. RB 19.

13. RB 2.

14. *Adhuc operibus servantes saeculo fidem, mentiri Deo per tonsuram noscuntur* (RB 52).

15. RB 52.

16. By imitating the Lord (RB 7).

17. *Venite, inquit. Quo? Ad me, Veritatem* (Hum 2.3).

18. SC 50.8 [CF 31:37].

19. *Rejicientes . . . caetera omnia quae puritati regulae adversabantur. Sicque rectitudinem regulae supra cunctum vitae tenorem ducentes, tam in ecclesiasticis quam in caeteris observationibus, regulae vestigiis sunt adaequati seu conformati. Exuti ergo veterem hominem, novum se induisse gaudebant* (*Little Exordium,* 15. Nom., p. 62) [EP 15.2–4; NLTEC 434].

20. *De Trinitate,* 4.6.7.

21. *Vita vestra est abscondita cum Christo in Deo* (Col 3:3).

22. *Passionibus Christi per patientiam , participemus* (RB, Prol.).

23. *Simplicitas justorum diriget eos.* "The simplicity of the just shall guide them" (Prv 11:3).

24. *Sed et si quid paululum restrictius, dictante aequitatis ratione, propter emendationem vitiorum, vel conservationem caritatis processerit . . .* "But if, following the dictates of the rule of equity, we go so far as to be somewhat rigorous, for the sake of correcting vices or preserving charity . . ." (RB, Prol.).

25. "True compunction," we read in a treatise attributed to St. Bernard, "is a precious treasure, an ineffable joy to the heart." *Bona compunctio thesaurus est desiderabilis, et inenarrabile gaudium in mente hominis* (*De Modo bene Vivendi,* ch. 10). The fact is, that compunction is born of love, and begets more love: and the love of God is the source of the only genuine joy. We are not sorry of an opportunity to expatiate at some length on the subject of compunction because that virtue is so intimately connected with the simplicity of St. Benedict's spirituality. Since, as Bossuet said, his holy Rule is "nothing more than a summary of Christianity, and an outline of the doctrines of the Gospel," he could not fail to give compunction the place in it which it must have in all truly Christian life. St. Benedict uses compunction to bring his disciple to humility, purity of heart, renunciation, and thus to the full flowering of the infused virtues and the Gifts of the Holy Ghost.

Compunction is one of the elements of custody of the heart. Beginning with the prologue, and then going on to several of the instruments of good works (especially the fifty-eighth), and to the more important passages of the seventh chapter, on humility, we find that the saint ranks compunction as one of the most formidable weapons in the spiritual combat. When he comes to speak of mental prayer (RB 20), Lent (RB 49), the oratory of the monastery (RB 52), he keeps returning to his beloved compunction. In the school of the Divine Office, the true disciple of St. Benedict cannot help but progress in the spirit of compunction.

26. The liturgy is the very life of the Church, her life as Spouse and as Mother; it is the great sacramental through which all souls can participate in all the phases of the life of Christ. It would be absurd to talk as if the liturgy and private prayer could be opposed to one another. On the one hand, from the point of view of contemplation, the *Opus Dei* is the most perfect formation for mental prayer, while, on the other, in the order of the virtue of religion, private prayer like constant vigilance (*vigilate semper*) tends to prepare the soul for a worthy participation in the sovereign work of the liturgy, which acts as distributor for the charity of the Church. So writes Jacques Maritain, summing up the thoughts of Fr. Clerissac, O.P., in his preface to the remarkable little book *The Mystery of the Church* (English translation published by Sheed and Ward).

27. In this connection read Dom Godefroid Belorgey, O.C.R., "*Pratique de 1'Oraison Mentale*"—Vol. 1, pp. 50–53. —*Translator*

28. *Little Exordium*, 15. Nom., p. 62 [EP 15.2; NLTEC 434].

29. In the summer time, there were two meals a day, at Sext (noon) and in the evening. During the fasts of the order, beginning September 14 and lasting until the stricter fast of Lent, there was only one meal daily, taken in the middle of the afternoon. In Lent, the single meal was after Vespers. The present-day *collation*, taken in the evening during the winter season and Lent in place of supper, is erroneously named. The word *collation* strictly refers to the reading before Compline in the chapter room. In the golden age of the order there was no collation, but *biberes*, that is, the monks repaired to the refectory and were served a drink to sustain them until the following afternoon, but nothing to eat. *Mixt*, the equivalent of breakfast, was unknown for the community at large, but was served some time before the regular meal to the servants of the refectory and the reader at table, as well as to the infirm. Today, in the strict observance, mixt is served in summer, and is replaced in winter by *frustulum*, for those who care to take it. In Lent, we take nothing in the morning. —*Translator*

30. *Little Exordium*, 15, Nom., p. 62 [EP 15.8; NLTEC 435].

31. RB 47.

32. Ibid.

33. RB 35. St. Benedict intended that each monk take his turn to do the cooking. Our fathers kept fairly closely to this practice,

although in large communities individuals were not expected to provide for two or three hundred brethren single-handed, cf. *Consuetudines*, ch. 108, Guignard, p. 225. —*Translator*

34. Cf. the works of Henri Pirenne on the economic history of the period. —*Translator*

35. *Little Exordium*, 15, Nom., p. 63 [EP 15.10; NLTEC 435].

36. These granges were in many respects like small monasteries, having oratories and all the other regular places, but no monks lived there permanently. They were tenanted by a small community of lay brothers under the command of one of their number called the *grangiarius* or grange master. At harvest time, the monks might be sent to a grange for several days at a time, and dormitories were kept in readiness for them on such occasions. *Consuetudines*, 84. Guignard, p. 225. —*Translator*

37. *Simplex eris explicando te a mundo, implicando duplex eris.* Homily 2 in Job.

38. *Little Exordium*, 15, Nom. p. 63 [EP 15.12; NLTEC 435].

39. Holy Communion was given under both species in the order in the twelfth and early thirteenth century, but was then discontinued, as it was also throughout the Church, except that in our order, by special dispensation, the deacon and sub-deacon continued to communicate under both kinds at the conventual High Mass. —*Translator*

40. Since this official pamphlet was written not merely as a speculative treatise for the satisfaction of a certain justifiable curiosity about our past, but with an intensely practical purpose, namely that of encouraging our communities to examine themselves in their practice of these fundamentals of Cistercian spirituality, without which we cannot fully carry out the task assigned to us in the Church by God, and reach the degree of sanctity he destines for us, it would be well to clarify the problem of liturgical simplicity by restating it in its modern context.

This can be done quite simply. There is no question for us of returning to the "one iron candlestick" of the first Cistercians. But we are *obliged* by the spirit of our vocation to resist the influx of showy and useless decorations into our sanctuaries. There is no longer any danger of gold and silver chalices: but our churches and liturgy are more spoiled than many of us realize by tawdry and garish imitations of gold and jewelry by pastiche and by an accumulation of vestments, carpets, curtains, statues, and stained glass which offend by their mixture of cheapness and garish display.

The problem is, then, not to try and get rid of all decorations as such: but to clear away all that is excessive and useless, to rid our altars and sanctuaries of bad art and, above all, to exercise discretion in choosing vestments, chalices, and other articles that breathe a spirit of simple piety instead of a semi-worldly atmosphere of theatrical display. All this is, however, complicated in our day by poverty itself: for it is a paradox of our time that it is the most inexpensive articles that often go to the greatest extremes of garishness, and these things are often all that we can afford. Finally, since most of these things come to the monks as gifts, they are at the mercy of the taste of their benefactors. —*Translator*

41. *Ne quid in domo Dei, in qua die ac nocte Deo devote servire cupiebant, remaneret, quod superbiam aut superfluitatem redoleret, aut paupertatem custodem virtutum, quam sponte elegerant, aliquando corrumperet, confirmaverunt ne retinerent cruces aureas seu argenteas, nisi tantummodo ligneas coloribus depictas, neque candelabra nisi unum ferreum . . .* (*Little Exordium*, 17, Nom. p. 64) [EP 17.5–6; NLTEC 438].

42. It is doubtful whether outsiders often attended Divine Office in the churches of our order. Special chapels were reserved for guests at the gatehouse. (See plan No. 45 of Marcel Aubert, *L'Architecture Cistercienne en France* [Paris, 1947].) —*Translator*

43. *Scimus quod illi, sapientibus et insipientibus debitores cum sint, carnalis populi devotionem, quia spiritualibus non possunt, corporalibus excitant ornamentis* (Apo. 12.28.) [CF 1:64].

44. If anyone would like to see a flagrant example of what a Cistercian church should not be, let him look at photographs of the baroque choir stalls, ceiling, etc., of the monastery church of Oliva (Prussia). Another offender is Hautecombe (Savoy). These may be contrasted with models of Cistercian restraint and purity like Fontenay, Aiguebelle, Fontfroide, Fossanova. Sénanque, Noirlac, Léoncel, etc. —*Translator*

45. EM 1.27; CF 72:106.

46. The celebrated story of St. Bernard traveling to the Grande Chartreuse on a richly caparisoned horse lent him by a Benedictine uncle of his, without even noticing all the showy trappings until they were politely drawn to his attention by the somewhat scandalized Carthusians, should be remembered in this connection. And we may remark that it is no legend, but a detail of unassailable authenticity, presented by his learned and saintly secretary and constant companion, Blessed Geoffrey of Auxerre, a most careful and scrupulously objective biographer (*Vita Bernardi Prima*, 3.4) [CF 76:149–150]. —*Translator*

47. This pure Gothic chasuble is a very important piece of evidence in the history of the liturgy, because of its authentic design—it

is simply a large, completely circular piece of cloth with a hole for the head to pass through. —*Translator*

48. The *Apologia de Guillelmum Abbatum* is one of the most important documents in a controversy between the Cistercians and Cluniac-Benedictines concerning their various interpretations of the Rule of St. Benedict. St. Bernard shows no mercy to the abuses that had crept into the Cluniac system, especially in the matter of diet, lavishness in the liturgy, and excessive worldliness. But the modern reader must also be reminded that all this was qualified, on St. Bernard's part, by an intimate friendship and deep love not only for many Benedictine abbots, but for the Cluniacs as a whole. It can never be said that, while he drew attention to isolated abuses, he was accusing the congregation as such of total decadence—or that the abuses themselves which he criticizes were gravely scandalous. The famous tirades against Cluny in the *Apologia* should never be read out of their context: and they follow several chapters of acknowledgments and qualifications. Blessed William of Saint Thierry, at whose instigation the *Apologia* was written, was himself, at the time, a Cluniac abbot, and he was only able to enter the Cistercian order against the express wish of St. Bernard, who wanted him to stay at Saint Thierry and reform his own order from within. St. Bernard was just as strong in castigating Cistercians, who were bordering on Pharisaism in their contempt of Cluny, as the easy-going Cluniacs themselves. —*Translator*

49. *Dicite pauperes, si tamen pauperes, in sancto quid facit aurum? . . . Quid, putas, in his omnibus quaeritur? Poenitentium compunctio, an intuentium admiratio* (Apo. 12.28). Writers like G. G. Coulton, who have called this reaction on the part of the Cistercians "puritanism," cannot justify their use of that term, at least in the strict sense. The puritans would never have admitted the concepts of monastic poverty and the mystical life with which this spirit of simplicity was essentially connected, cf. Etienne Gilson, *Mystical Theology of St. Bernard*, p. 233. —*Translator*

50. Ernald of Bonnevaux, *Vita Bernardi Prima*, 2.6 [CF 76:84–85].

51. *Omitto oratoriorum immensas altitudines, immoderatas longitudines, supervacuas latitudines, sumptuosas depolitiones, curiosas depictiones; quae dum orantium in se retorquent aspectum, impediunt et affectum, et mihi quodammodo repraesentant antiquum ritum Judaeorum* (Apo. 12.28) [CF 1:63–64].

52. This tenet, which is one of the fundamental precepts of twentieth-century architecture, was *consciously* anticipated in the monasteries of the Cistercian order by about eight hundred years. This

accounts for the fact that modernistic lines, reinforced concrete and glass have entered so effectively into the construction or reconstruction of certain monasteries in Europe (vg. Clairfontaine, a convent of Trappistine nuns in Belgium). The architecture of our day is more eminently suited to Cistercian spirituality than any style that has been devised since the art of the great twelfth- and thirteenth-century Cistercian builders was forgotten. In fact, when Cistercians build in fake, over-decorated Gothic in preference to something on simple, functional modern lines, they are unconsciously contradicting the whole Cistercian tradition and ideal in their very attempt to preserve it. On the other hand, the more functional and the less antiquarian our use of Gothic styles, the more true will they be to the spirit of the purest Cistercian art. —*Translator*

53. A well-known painter, Horace Vernet, expressed the same sort of enthusiasm as Montalembert when, on the occasion of a procession at our monastery at Staouéli in Algeria, he observed the effects of light and shade, on the coarse wool of the Cistercian cowls. "When it comes to downright good taste," he said, "what have modern religious habits to offer in comparison to the austere cowls of your professed monks, or even the cloaks of your lay brothers?" He believed he could see the spirit of our founders in the very simplicity of our monastic garb.

54. The nations here listed follow the chronological order of the foundations of the first monasteries mentioned under each heading.

4. Anxiety to Preserve Simplicity

1. Nom., p. 214. *Hucusque capitula de institutione primorum monachorum Cisterciensium, et de Carta Caritatis fere omnia sunt sumpta* [NLTEC 454].

2. *Quia dum talibus intenditur, utilitas bonae meditationis vel disciplina religiosae gravitatis saepe negligitur* (Nom., p. 217) [Instituta 20; NLTEC 464].

3. *Panis ibi autopyrus pro simila, pro careno sapa, pro rhombis olera, pro quibuslibet deliciis legumina ponebantur* (*Vita Bernardi Prima*, 2. 6. Migne, *Patrologia Latina*, 185, col. 272b) [CF 76:85].

4. Nom., p. 279.

5. It had been founded by St. Louis. As to the punishment with which the abbot was threatened, deprivation of wine may sound incongruous to American ears, but one must remember the ineradicable conviction of the whole French nation that plain water is a menace to health. —*Translator*

6. *Quae deformant antiquam ordinis honestatem et paupertati nostrae non congruunt. . . . Superfluitates et curiositates notabiles in sculpturis et aedificiis, pavimentis et aliis similibus interdicimus* (Nom., 287).

7. Nom., 272. There was, as a matter of fact, both in the twelfth and thirteenth centuries, a flourishing Cistercian school of poets, in houses both in England and France, including Rievaulx (St. Aelred's abbey) in Yorkshire, Ford in Devon, and Froidmont in the diocese of Beauvais, where Blessed Helinand, a converted troubadour, continued to write in French. St. Bernard himself has been named as the author of many beautiful hymns, especially the *Jesu dulcis memoria*, used on the feast of the Holy Name in the Roman as well as in the Cistercian Breviary. A possible explanation for this statute against poets is the fact that a misguided Cistercian of the abbey of Pairis, near Basel, wrote a long and pompous epic in praise of Frederic Barbarossa, whom the order had been fighting almost unanimously for over twenty years, defending the Holy See against Frederic's various antipopes. —*Translator*

8. *Histoire abrégée de l'ordre de Cîteaux*, p. 45.

9. *L'âge de vermeil*: literally, silver gilt age.

10. The phrase *paupertas semper, sordes nunquam* (always poor but never dirty), applied to St. Bernard in his love for cleanliness, did not militate against a two-months' beard. Of course, only lay brothers were permitted to cultivate a good long beard.

11. This move of the Holy Father's was perhaps instigated by the same abbot (Stephen of Lexington) who, three years before had acted *motu proprio*, without the consent of the General Chapter, to get Innocent IV to authorize, directly, the establishment of the College of St. Bernard at Paris. We may presume that this abbot had concealed, from the Holy Father, the fundamental law of the Charter of Charity, by which even St. Stephen himself had been bound: "Let no church and no person of our order ask of anyone whatever any privilege contrary to the common institutions of our order, or make use of such privilege if it has been obtained" (Carta Char., Nom., p. 69) [CC 10; NLTEC 500].

12. *Ad preces et admonitionem Sanctissimi Patris nostri Summi Pontificis, qui super hoc scripsit Capitulo Generali, statuitur . . .* (Nom., 396).

13. *Supellex talis sit, ut statui paupertatis, quam professi sunt monachi, conveniat; nihil superflui in ea sit* (Nom., p. 597, No. 19, in fine). *Omnes, tam abbates quam monachi, pannis nigri et albi dumtaxat coloris simplicibus . . . vestiantur, sic ut nihil in eis appareat quod novitates saecularium sapiat* (Ibid., pp. 599–600, No. 28).

14. *Aureum opus, parvum mole, sed pondere et pretio satis magnum* (Annal. Cisterc., t. 1, p. 120, No. 10).

5. *Let Us Die in Our Simplicity*

1. *Una caritate, una regula, similisque vivamus moribus* [CC 3.2; NLTEC 444].

2. That of 1924. The same chapter also called for a series of lives of the Cistercian saints, and for monographs on the monasteries of the order. —*Translator*

3. *Omnibus nobis nulla virtus magis necessaria quam simplicitas verecunda* (S. Cyril., De Orat., 8).

4. *Dura et aspera per quae itur ad Deum.*

5. *Cum gaudio Sancti Spiritus offerat Deo. . . .*

6. *Communicantes Christi passionibus gaudete* (1 Pt 4:13).

7. Sg 1:16. "The spouse calls her beloved a little bundle, since her love leads her to consider as light all the trials and sufferings that have been prepared for her . . . not that the divine bundle is light in itself, but it is light to a heart that loves. So, too, the spouse not only says, 'My beloved is a bundle of myrrh,' but she adds, 'to me,' *mihi*, who love. And she calls him 'my beloved,' *dilectus meus*, to show that the power of her love overcomes all bitterness and that love is as strong as death *fortis est ut mors dilectio* [Sg 8:6] (SC 43.1).

"She will not feel her wounds as long as she keeps her eyes fixed upon those of her Master. She does not lose all her feelings—she overcomes them. Pain is there, but she has risen above pain, and condemns it" (SC 61.7–8).

8. *Non jam timore gehennae sed amore Christi et consuetudine ipsa bona et delectatione virtutum, quae Dominus iam in operario suo mundo a vitiis et peccatis, Spiritu Sancto dignabitur demonstrare.* "No longer moved by the fear of hell, but by the love of Christ and by the good habit he has acquired and by the consolation in the practice of virtue, all of which God will be pleased to show forth, through the Holy Spirit, in his servant who has been purified of his vices and sins" (RB 7).

9. First Sermon on the Feast of St. Andrew, paragraph 5.

10. *O bona ac beata simplicitas, quae quibusdam inest naturaliter. Longe tamen illa beatior et excellentior, quae laboribus et sudoribus ex malitia tradita es. . . . Altissimae humilitatis et mansuetudinis gentrix et altrix est. . . . Numquam videns simplicitatem ab humilitate separatam* (Scal. Parad., Grad. 24).

11. Homily 72 on Matthew.

12. St. Basil, Constit. Monast. 30; Patrologia Graeca, 31:1419. St. Benedict refers to St. Basil as "our Father St. Basil" in order to emphasize, for our benefit, the importance of this holy doctor's writings on the monastic life. John Cassian prescribed the same simplicity in order that everything liable to feed the spirit of vanity or pride might be obviated. And our father St. Bernard declared that "whatever is superfluous in external things is a sign of vanity within."

13. Homily 83 in Matthew.

14. Homily 68 in Matthew.

15. Apostolic Constitution, "*Umbratilem*," July 8, 1924 (Act. Apost. Sed. 16, p. 385 sq.).

16. *Jam nos alias eos commemoravimus, qui ad regularium vitam adstricti in Ecclesia assiduo precum macerationumque officio funguntur.*

17. *Qui ab societate hominum sejuncti prorsus in omnem vitam ac segregati ut aeternam eorum salutem occulto quodam tacitoque apostolatu tueantur in cellae quisque suae solitudine sic degunt, ut illinc nullo anni tempore discedant.*

18. The way in which the Holy Father places side by side the notions of "simplicity" and "holy rusticity" recall Bossuet's words addressed to the Savior adored in Bethlehem by the shepherds: "Your example is a command. And what does it command? *Simplicity*—and, if I may be so bold as to say it—a certain *holy rusticity* in these new adorers which the angel has brought to Your crib" (*Elévations sur les Mystères*, 16e semaine, 7e élévation).

19. *Ideoque et nos tantam habentes impositam nubem testium, deponentes omne pondus . . . per patientiam curramus ad propositum nobis certamen, aspicientes in auctorem fidei, et consummatorem Jesum* (Heb 12:1–2).

Part 2
Text 1. Our Original Simplicity

1. Statements like this one occur very frequently in all the works of St. Bernard and they give us the very core of his doctrine of humility. The reason he insists so much on self-knowledge is not merely that we may be convinced of our "vileness." Humility is truth, and our vileness is only half of the truth. The other half is our greatness: our likeness to, our capacity for union with God. *But he is, and will ever remain, infinitely above us, and in his sight we are always as nothing.*

2. The brute-animals, having no rational soul, do not have this perfection of simplicity, and they will never be able to ascend to the blessedness of participation in the Divine Life, God's own vision and love of his own infinitely simple reality.

3. The saint is not here accusing all men of conscious and deliberate hypocrisy. What he means will be clear from the example of Adam and Eve: fallen man seeks, by a perverse quasi-instinct, which he has acquired with the Fall and which the saint calls duplicity, to conceal from himself, from other men, and from God the truth about himself: his own insufficiency in himself, his utter dependence on God for everything. There is always in fallen man this persistent tendency to make himself like unto God, to put himself in the place of God, that is, to make his own ego the center of the universe.

4. Once again, we are gravitating about the fundamental paradox on which is based St. Bernard's whole theory of humility. We are at once great, and nothingness. The greatness in ourselves is God's work; the evil, the vileness, is the work we have done with our own will, in direct contradiction to our own nature as it was created by God. Cf. St. Benedict, RB 4. *Bonum aliquod in se cum viderit Deo applicet et non sibi, malum vero semper a se factum sciat et sibi reputet.* Let the monk attribute whatever good he finds in himself to God and not to himself, but let him know that the evil is always his own work, and let him attribute it to himself.

5. For their own sake, as ends, not means. The saint is now discussing the corruption of our immortality by death, which is parallel to the contradiction generated within us between simplicity and duplicity. We are immortal, and yet we die. The ultimate of this contradiction is the eternal living death of hell. Our mortality is connected with the love of earthly things, *quae quidem omnia ad interitum sunt,* for they are all destined to perish.

6. *Sapit:* literally, knows as it were by tasting. Hence *Sapientia,* wisdom, is the knowledge of God by the experience of (tasting) his infinite goodness.

7. In other words: the being, the reality of material things is unstable and impermanent. Therefore the soul, loving these things, becomes itself unstable, vacillating, weak, confused, as the saint will show in the next paragraph.

8. *Fruendo mortalibus mortalitatem se induit.* . . . The verb *frui,* in the Fathers of the Church and the Scholastics, has a special meaning beyond the ordinary one: "to enjoy." It is the precise technical term used to describe the act of the will resting in the possession of something as in its last end. Hence, properly speaking, the only object of *frui* for the human soul is God himself. We may try to possess creatures in this way, but our attempt is necessarily doomed to failure. It is a metaphysical impossibility. Creatures are for our use (*uti*) as means to lead us to "fruition" in God.

9. The implications of this are very far-reaching. The goodness, beauty, usefulness, etc., of material creation have a definite purpose: to bring men to God, and in a wider sense to be used by all living beings for their own good. If, then, we desire to *possess* any part of this goodness and beauty for ourselves alone, we automatically enter into competition with all the other beings for whose use it was created. This, then, in addition to the natural instability of material things, is a second source of unrest, the second great source of *fear*. In connection with our topic, simplicity, it is also evident that these desires are in many ways causes of *multiplicity in the soul*. The very multiplicity of material objects multiplies our desires. The multiplicity of competitors, real and *imaginary*, multiplies our fears. The soul that loves material things finds simple recollection impossible: it is constantly tortured by a thousand images, specters, phantasms, hopes, fears, loves, hatreds, etc.

10. The saint here treats of the third of the three parallel disfigurements of the three elements of likeness to God in the soul. Simplicity was "overlaid" by duplicity, immortality by death, now liberty is similarly obscured, though left essentially intact, by slavery to an inordinate desire of material things—i.e., to sin.

11. This sentence is a perfect description of the state of *interior simplicity* as treated in the first section of the report. The soul is said to desire *nothing* because, in such a state, it is united to God and possesses him, although in another sense its love for him is always a mixture of satisfaction and desire, even in heaven. It is said to fear nothing, because its absolute confidence in God (*fiducia* is extremely important in the mysticism of St. Bernard, and therefore an essential ingredient in Cistercian simplicity) precludes all servile fear.

12. Ps 108:29. This psalm is traditionally interpreted as referring to Judas, in whom duplicity went to its greatest limit—the attempt to betray God into the hands of death! St. Bernard is not concerned with Judas in this passage.

13. It is interesting to compare this passage with a fundamental text of St. John of the Cross, who often greatly resembles St. Bernard. The great Carmelite says: "The reason why it is necessary for the soul in order to attain divine union with God, to pass through this dark night of mortification of the desires and denial of pleasures in all things, is because all the affections which it has for creatures are pure darkness in the eyes of God, *and when the soul is clothed in these affections, it has no capacity for being enlightened and possessed by the pure and simple light of God* if it cast them not first from it; for the light cannot agree with darkness. . . . It must be known that the affection and

attachment which the soul has for creatures renders it like to these creatures; and the greater is its affection, the closer is the equality and likeness between them, for love creates a likeness between that which loves and that which is loved. . . . And thus he that loves a creature becomes as low as is that creature, and in some ways lower: for love not only makes the lover equal to the object of his love but also subjects him to it. Wherefore in the same way it comes to pass that the soul that loves anything else becomes incapable of pure union with God and transformation in him" (*Ascent of Mount Carmel*, 1.4). (*Peers translation*)

14. Cf. Gilson, *Mystical Theology of St. Bernard*, p. 67ff.

Text 2. Intellectual Simplicity: Humility Is Truth

1. *Hinc egregia creatura gregi admixta est.* . . .

2. Cf. The internal contradiction in man since the Fall as expressed in the previous texts.

3. The result of the Fall was a quasi-natural duplicity, super-imposed on the simple nature of man. But one of the chief causes of the Fall was, according to the saint in this passage, the failure of man to consider the truth of his essential contingency upon God—a dependence which is his greatest glory, and the source of all his freedom. Consequently, culpable ignorance of the source of all the goods proper to his nature was the cause of all man's sorrows, and, likewise, the cause of the duplicity which keeps him a prisoner of weakness, darkness, mortality, suffering, and sin. *But the first step in the recovery of our simplicity is the acknowledgment of the truth*: this truth has two aspects. The first, as we have just seen, is the truth about ourselves.

4. "Hope of salvation" is not here used as a more or less general expression (equivalent to "you cannot be saved"). The knowledge of God, of his goodness and his mercy, effectually begets hope in our souls, to counterbalance the fear generated by knowledge of our own helplessness. As the argument develops, it becomes apparent that knowledge of ourselves without knowledge of God *only begets despair*.

5. *Plenitudo legis est charitas* (Rom 13:10).

6. The text which space obliges us to omit, comprising most of the last two sections of Sermon 37, contains some excellent rules for the practice of humility, in which the saint explains why it is always safer to place ourselves lower than we really are, although the ideal would be to think of ourselves exactly as we are, neither better nor worse, if we only knew how we and others stand in the eyes of God.

7. St. Bernard, like many others attracted to the Cistercian cloister in his time (cf. St. Aelred, William of Saint Thierry, Alan of Lille,

Blessed Guerric, etc.), belonged to the intellectual aristocracy of the twelfth century.

8. It is interesting to note that the Latin word here is simplex, simple. The simplicity of those who are merely ignorant is never proposed as an ideal by the early Cistercians and, in this place, St. Bernard takes it for granted that they should be instructed by the learned, and that there should be learned men to instruct them. But it is not everybody's vocation to be a learned man, just as it would be better if no one passed his whole life in that form of "simplicity" which is mere ignorance.

9. *Quia tu repulisti scientiam, repellam et ego te, ut non fungaris mihi sacerdotio* (Hos 4:6).

10. *Qui autem docti fuerint, fulgebunt quasi splendor firmamenti; et qui ad justitiam erudiunt multos, quasi stellae in perpetuas aeternitates* (Dn 12:3).

11. *Scientia inflat* (1 Cor 8:1).

12. *Qui apponit scientiam, apponit dolorem.* Persius, Ecc 1:18. This is not the only time when the saint paradoxically quotes a pagan poet in the midst of a passage where he is showing the vanity of secular culture.

13. Cf. St. Bonaventure, 2 Sent. D. 23, a. 2. Q. 3 ad 4. *Amor multo plus se extendit quam visio . . . ubi deficit intellectus ibi proficit affectus.* The Seraphic Doctor was inspired by St. Bernard in this passage, cf. St. Bernard, *De Consideratione*, 5.14.30 [CF 37:177–178]; De Div., 4.3 [CF 68:31–32].

14. Op. cit., 5.14. 30 [CF 37:177–178].

15. *Sanctum facit affectio sancta.*

16. *Unigenitus Dei Filius* (March 19, 1924).

17. SC 69.2.

18. Any soul that makes account of all its knowledge and ability in order to come to union with God is supremely ignorant in the eyes of God and will remain far removed from that vision (St. John of the Cross, *Ascent of Mount Carmel*, 1. 4. Peers tr., vol. 1, p. 26).

19. St. Bernard says that the evidence of God in his creation, so visible even to natural reason alone without grace, is sufficient to oblige men to a complete and uncompromising *natural* love of God above all else (*De Diligendo Deo*, 2.6) [CF 13:98]. For the ascent of the mind to God through creatures, see especially St. Bonaventure, *Itinerarium Mentis in Deum*, 1.15. *"Aperi igitur oculos tuos, aures spirituales admove, labia tua solve et cor tuum appone ut IN OMNIBUS CREATURIS DEUM TUUM VIDEAS, AUDIAS, LAUDES, DILIGES ET COLES, MAGNIFICAS ET HONORES, ne forte totus contra te orbis terrarum*

consurgat." To ignore the voice of creatures crying out to us the glory of their Creator draws down upon us a terrible fate!

20. SC 8.5.

21. He does not mean that they ought to have known of the Incarnation of Christ before it happened, and by natural reason alone: both would be impossible. But they should have recognized in God the *goodness* that would eventually show itself in Christ's birth and his death for us on the cross.

22. *Non possum ego a meipso facere quidquam* (Jn 5:30). "For if any man think himself to be something, whereas he is nothing, he deceiveth himself" (Gal 6:3).

23. *De gradibus humilitatis et superbiae,* 10.28–30 [CF 13:57–59].

24. "Not to be more wise than it behooveth to be wise" (Rom 12:3).

25. Dil 2.4: *Utrumque ergo scias necesse est, et quid sis et quid a teipso non sis: ne aut omnino non glorieris, aut inaniter glorieris. . . . Homo factus in honore, cum honorem ipsum non intelligit, talis suae ignorantiae merito comparatur pecoribus.*

26. For the details of the action by which the Word teaches the soul self-knowledge and draws it on to interior simplicity, see Hum 7.20–21 [CF 13:47–50].

27. St. Bernard would agree with St. Bonaventure that God is nevertheless present to the soul through some effect created in the soul by himself, not in the absence of all media whatever. That effect is love (Div 4.2. cf. St. Bonaventure, 2 Sent., D. 23, a 2, q. 3).

28. SC 31.6.

Text 3. Simplification of the Will: Obedience

1. Cf. Sermon 3 on the Circumcision. After describing the virtue of discretion as it is found in the highest degree of sanctity, and which sees through all the artifices of the demon and of our own pride, St. Bernard concludes that this virtue is a "rare bird" on earth, but assures his monks that its place is amply filled by simple obedience, which he describes thus: *ut nihil plus, nihil minus, nihil aliter quam imperatum sit faciatis.*

2. Cf. 1 Sm 15, and St. Bernard Sermon 33 on the Canticle of Canticles, paragraph ten, on those who indulge in self-chosen mortifications, cf. St. John of the Cross, *Ascent of Mount Carmel,* 1.8, 4–5.

3. Cf. RB 7, eighth degree of humility. Also, Dom Godefroid Belorgey *L'Humilité Bénédictine,* pp. 243–250.

4. This strong Cistercian emphasis on fraternal union in the Spirit of Love (*Deus Caritas est!*) is nowhere more strikingly evident

than in the document which is the very legal foundation of the order, the *Carta Caritatis*. The very title tells us so, and meditation of the first two pages will make it clear in no uncertain terms. This, indeed, is the whole basis for Cistercian simplicity, i.e., for the unity of charity and mutual forbearance in following one rule, one set of usages.

5. It would certainly be a grave error to say that all our desires were evil. The saint makes it perfectly clear that self-will is only to be applied to desires in rebellion against, in conflict with the will of God: and when our neighbor is in open rebellion against God, it is also God's will for us to resist him. Cf. *De Praecepto et Dispensatione*, 4.9–10.

6. This is to be taken in the sense that self-will itself is the object on which the flames of hell feed, not merely that it is the efficient cause of the flames of hell feeding on some other matter, viz. our bodies.

7. We remind the reader of the contents of the first text quoted, in order to obviate the misinterpretation of these lines. Self-will belongs to the layer of corruption superinduced upon our true nature, upon our true freedom of will. It must be consumed before we can really become *ourselves*. Until then, it and it alone is the reason for our sufferings.

8. Cf. *De Praecepto et Dispensatione*, 10.23: "It is a sign of an imperfect soul and of a very infirm will to argue insistently against the decisions of superiors . . . to demand a reason for every little thing, and to look with suspicion on every order the reason for which is not immediately apparent, and never to obey willingly except when you are told to do something you like to do, etc."

9. RB 71–72.

10. Dil 2.

11. To cite two other texts: St. Bernard, *De Praecepto et Dispensation*, 10.23–24; St. Aelred, *Speculum Charitatis*, 2.3–4.

12. St. Bernard, Miss 4: *"Fiat" est desiderii indicium. . . .*

Text 4. Simplification of the Will: Our Own Judgment

1. *Idololatriae scelus est non acquiescere, et quasi peccatum ariolandi repugnare* (1 Sm 15:23). The reference is to Saul's self-chosen sacrifice, against the express command of God.

2. The whole sermon should be studied carefully. It is a good exposition of the purgative way, according to Cistercian asceticism: the stress being on *obedience and fraternal charity* as two most essential prerequisites for the reception of graces of infused prayer.

3. He sums up the dispositions required for intimate union with God in the following list: piety, peace, meekness, justice, obedience, joyfulness (*hilaritas*), and humility.

4. Cf. Lk 2:46–51.

5. "*Mutuae pacis futurum praecaventes naufragium . . .*" (*Carta Caritatis*, Guignard, p. 79) [CC Prol. 3; NLTEC 442].

6. This is especially stressed in St. Bernard's Hum 5 and 7.

7. *Jerusalem quae aedificatur ut civitas, cujus participatio ejus in idipsum* (Ps 121:3) is one of the most perplexing lines in the Psalms. What is the meaning of this "selfsame"? For St. Bernard, it is simply the *voluntas communis* or charity: the identical love of one object, *God's will*—and this love unites all the blessed among themselves as well as to him.

8. By the words *idipsum sentiamus* (think the same) St. Bernard does not prescribe a stereotyped uniformity *of* thought, but a charitable agreement between differences of opinion springing from all the inevitable variety in temperament, background, education, etc., which it would be folly to try and destroy.

9. It must not be forgotten that the precise meaning of the word *separate* here is to set one's self apart from others, in one's own estimation, by pride, self-esteem, self-congratulation, attachment to one's own opinion or one's own will. It means to say with the Pharisee: "*Non sum sicut caeteri homines.*" Pride is the root of all schisms and heresies.

Text 5. *Perfect Simplicity: Unity of Spirit with God*

1. On the importance of fiducia, confidence, cf. especially Sermon 83 on the Canticle of Canticles. This virtue is absolutely essential if the soul is to pass through the grueling purification by the truth, that is, by an ever clearer and clearer knowledge of the hideous deformity that has been wrought on God's image, within her, by sin. Only perfect confidence in God's merciful love can draw the soul on toward him in spite of what she has realized about herself.

2. There are four degrees of love for the monk in this tract on the love of God. The first is that well-regulated self-love by which we love ourselves enough to avoid the pains of hell and seek heaven. The second is when a man begins to love God because of the gifts and consolations God offers him. The third, the highest degree reached in this life by many of the most spiritual men, is to love God for himself alone. The fourth, and most perfect degree, reached in this life only by a few great saints (the fewness is not God's fault, but men's) is

to love ourselves for the sake of God. All souls attain to this if and when they reach heaven.

3. *Tamquam vas perditum* (Ps 30:13).

4. *Defecit caro mea et cor meum, Deus cordis mei, et pars mea, Deus in aeternum* (Ps 72:26).

5. Man is made for this perfect union with God. Capacity for it is in his nature itself. That is, this union is within the scope of our *obediential potency*, to be deduced by the direct action of God on the basis of our cooperation with grace. God does not create beings with a potency for ends which they can never attain. Hence, according to St. Bernard, the fact that by our very essence we are capable of this perfect union with God in love means that all men can attain it, if they will freely cooperate with God's love drawing them to him. See SC 83.2. Also the article "Transforming Union in St. Bernard and St. John of the Cross," in the *Collectanea*, O.C.R., April 1, 1943.

6. Since God's will is the perfect beatification of the soul, the two are, materially speaking, the same thing. But the formal reason of the soul's happiness is to be found in the fact that this happiness is God's will, not that it is the soul's own happiness.

One of the leading Catholic figures at the turn of the twentieth century, **Jean-Baptiste Chautard, O.C.S.O.** (1858–1935), was a French Trappist abbot and religious writer. He was integral in the expansion of his Cistercian Order, even achieving the purchase of Cîteaux Abbey in France, where Cistercianism began around 1100. Chautard was later responsible for new foundations in Belgium and Latin America. He is best known for his book *The Soul of the Apostolate*, which has been translated into many languages. Several popes have recommended Chautard's work, including Pope emeritus Benedict XVI, who cited it during his visit to Lourdes in 2008.

Thomas Merton (1915–1968) is widely acclaimed as one of the most influential spiritual masters of the twentieth century. A Trappist monk of the Abbey of Gethsemani, Kentucky, he was a poet, social activist, and student of comparative religion. In 1949, he was ordained to the priesthood and given the name Fr. Louis. Merton wrote more than seventy books, mostly on spirituality, social justice, and a quiet pacifism, as well as scores of essays and reviews, including his best-selling autobiography, *The Seven Storey Mountain*.